Selling Your Way IN.

FOREWORD BY **MIKE WEINBERG**

SELLING YOUR WAY IN

THE PLAYBOOK FOR
SETTING YOUR INCOME
AND OWNING YOUR LIFE

KRISTIE K. JONES

NEW YORK

LONDON • NASHVILLE • MELBOURNE • VANCOUVER

SELLING YOUR WAY IN

The Playbook for Setting Your Income and Owning Your Life

Published in New York, New York, by Morgan James Publishing. Morgan James is a trademark of Morgan James, LLC. www.MorganJamesPublishing.com

Proudly distributed by Publishers Group West®

ISBN 9781636983714 paperback
ISBN 9781636983721 ebook
Library of Congress Control Number:
2024932933

Cover and Interior Design by:
Chris Treccani
www.3dogcreative.net

Morgan James is a proud partner of Habitat for Humanity Peninsula and Greater Williamsburg. Partners in building since 2006.

Get involved today! Visit: www.morgan-james-publishing.com/giving-back

DEDICATION

To my parents.

Thank you for taking the huge professional risk to leave the safety of working for others into a life of entrepreneurship that was filled with financial uncertainty, professional challenges, and times of amazing success and abundance. Scott and I wouldn't be the confident, successful, and financially literate people we are today if we hadn't gotten our MBA nightly at the kitchen table. You modeled by doing, and I'm so grateful to have you both as role models.

To Scott.

There's no one I've enjoyed talking shop with over the years more than you. I'm so proud of what you've accomplished professionally and personally. I love you very much.

TABLE OF CONTENTS

FOREWORD

The book you are now holding is one of the most unique and powerful resources I have consumed in my thirty-four-year career.

Selling Your Way IN is not just a great book. And it is not just a must-read for anyone currently in sales seeking to take their game to the next level, or someone considering the life-changing career transition into professional selling. Kristie Jones has written a blueprint for success in life and sales.

From the introduction to the final chapter, you immediately know with 100 percent certainty that this book was written by a *real* person, who's lived a *real* life with *real* experiences, has experienced *real* success, and is on a mission to help others do the same. Kristie's personal stories are as captivating as they are valuable—and completely relatable to me as our career paths are eerily similar from our parents' mentoring to why we moved into sales, from how we progressed into leadership roles and eventually went out on our own into the "sales improvement" business.

I've had the privilege of watching Kristie's business and influence in the sales community rapidly expand over the past decade. When I am asked why she has been so successful, my answer is simple and direct: She is a master at making others successful. And this was her motivation for writing *Selling Your Way IN:* a desire to provide you with a behind-the-scenes peek at the makeup, mindset, disciplines, approaches, and actions of the top-ten percent of sales pros, the real sales rockstars who exceed quota, year after year—so you can become a sales Rock Star too!

Unless you are already the top salesperson in your industry, earning more money than you ever dared dream, this book is for you. I have consumed over fifty books on sales, and none were similar to *Selling Your Way IN*. Kristie's masterpiece is a refreshing reminder of why I got into sales in the first place and a powerful reinforcement why, to this day, I still proudly proclaim that I. Love. Sales.

If you're looking to experience the fun, the freedom, and yes, the financial rewards from becoming a top-producing superstar, grab a highlighter, pad, and pen and get ready to open your eyes, ears, mind, and heart for what Kristie has prepared for you. And while you will be tempted to consume her blueprint quickly because it's a fast read with entertaining stories and sage advice, my strong encouragement is to intentionally slow your roll. Don't rush through the pearls of wisdom that Kristie's years of experience enable her to share.

While the entire book offers practical value nugget after value nugget, the #Kristieisms in Chapter 3 are so packed with applicable life wisdom that they are worth the price of the book alone—my two favorites being #ownyourownincome and "hunters aren't helpers."

I promise this is one of those rare books that truly delivers on the promise of its subtitle, *The Playbook for Setting Your Income and Owning Your Life*. However, this promise comes with one critical caveat: you must digest and then apply Kristie's counsel in Section One . . . to *meet yourself* (and recognize your own style and tendencies) so you can position yourself in a sales role that plays to your strengths. Sales is not a one-size-fits-all career. You will have way more fun and experience faster and greater success by ensuring you get yourself into the *right seat* on the *sales bus*.

Once you've crafted your personal plan to maximize your sales career success and satisfaction, dive into Section Two, which offers a helpful big-picture view of the sales process, covering essential topics ranging from strategic targeting of accounts to, one of my favorites, sharpening your sales story (value proposition). These nuggets from Kristie are the essential building blocks for launching a highly effective new business development-focused sales initiative, and wise salespeople will adopt them as their own.

Finally, drink in the priceless life coaching from Section Three that will help you tie it all together. Learn how top producers view themselves, their jobs, and their customers while building disciplines into their life that keep them mentally, emotionally, and physically healthy so they consistently live and sell from an abundance mentality.

Wishing you all the fun, freedom, and financial rewards that accrue to the salesperson who masters the concepts presented in this wonderfully helpful, well-written book!

Mike Weinberg, author of *New Sales. Simplified, Sales Management. Simplified*, and *The First-Time Manager: Sales*

My Kitchen Table MBA

t isn't everyone who can say they got an education in sales at the dinner table, but for my brother and me, that's exactly where our education, and our love of sales, began. We both earned the equivalent of an MBA at the kitchen table.

My father was the owner and broker of a Coldwell Banker franchise, and my mother was a top agent. Our family dinner conversations often revolved around listings, out-of-town buyers, and commission checks. Money was a transparent topic in our family. We knew what each of my mother's commission checks were, what my dad paid himself, whether or not he was taking a paycheck, or if he was forgoing his own salary to make sure he was able to pay his employees. We even knew when his paycheck was going straight to the government to cover the taxes from my mother's income. When I say transparent, I mean *really* transparent. So from a very early age, my brother and I knew there was big money to be made in sales and more money as an individual contributor than as an owner or leader.

For my brother, those impromptu training sessions turned into a career as an extremely successful individual contributor. Me? I pursued other careers initially, until finally, I realized sales really was my first love and my true passion. What I also learned was that, unlike my brother, my joy isn't in building success through selling, but in building success for people who want to build their own success through selling.

Over the years, my brother and I have often discussed our different sales roles, how he followed our mom's path as an individual contributor and how I went the sales leadership route, following in our dad's footsteps. Both think the other is crazy and wouldn't change places under any circumstance. But what we both agree on is that if my dad hadn't made the decision in 1979 to quit his job with the United Telephone Company to partner with his brother in running the Century 21 Real Estate office, our lives would probably have been very different.

Our life before Dad made that decision and moved us to Topeka, Kansas, wasn't a bad life. But that decision to become a business owner afforded our family an even better life. My dad was making a fair salary as a mid-level manager with the telephone company, but my mom was a teacher working in rural schools where in some cases K-12 were all in one building, and none of the teachers made much money. She spent thirteen years as an underpaid employee before using her time off one summer to get her real estate license. That decision was a real game-changer for our family. She quit her job teaching and threw herself into selling real estate full time. She doubled her income in the first year.

Between my dad's savvy as a sales leader and manager and my mom's ability to outsell her competition, our family sold our way out of the life we had into a life that afforded us more financial freedom, bigger houses, and the ability to pay cash for cars and college, with enough left over for my parents to build a nice retirement account. All thanks to their choosing a profession in sales.

A sales career can do the same for you. You can sell your way out of an unfulfilling job, financial struggles, and a life of someone else controlling your income . . . and into a life of financial abundance, a rewarding job, and being in full control of your income.

If you're just now considering a career in sales, my hope is that by sharing my story, successes, and missteps and offering actionable tips and advice that I wish I'd learned earlier, you will find the confidence to leave the job you dread getting up for each day and consider a career in sales. I want this book to be a resource for how you can build a sales career to change your current professional situation into one that you've only dreamed about.

If you've already made the leap into a career in sales, my hope is that after reading this book, you'll have the courage to take your sales career to the next level by asking for that promotion you're not sure you're ready for or deciding to leave your current sales position or company for one with more personal growth and financial potential. Some of you may even decide that you'd rather use your sales skills to start your own business. I want each of these to be options for you.

That's why I wrote this book, because I know I am blessed to have had a different upbringing than most people, and as a result, I believe I have a responsibility to pass along my knowledge, advice, and encouragement to make it easier for you to navigate your way to the best possible outcome for you and your family.

I want to help you leverage a sales career, *your* sales career, to buy that dream house, take a vacation without worrying about how you'll pay it off long after the memories have started to fade, and see your kids graduate college debt-free, as my son did, and have a different life than most college grads today. All of this isn't just for "natural salespeople"; it can be a reality for anyone willing to learn and do the work. You *can* sell your way into a life that is more professionally, emotionally, and financially rewarding—filled with possibilities and opportunities. I want everyone to have the life they want, and by choosing a career in sales, I know that I can help you make that a reality.

BACKSTORY AND FOUNDATIONS

If you're holding this book, I'm going to assume you're already building your sales career or you're considering how to begin. But just in case you're experiencing doubts about whether you belong in sales, reading this book may help you discover that you don't have to fit the typical sales profile to have a meaningful, and lucrative, career as part of a sales team. In fact, some of the most successful sales reps I've worked with don't have a typical sales profile, but they have created their own success profile and plan. And that's exactly what I'm going to teach you to do here.

We All Start Somewhere

I didn't start out to be a sales professional or an entrepreneur. When someone asks me to tell my story of how I decided to start my business, they're usually surprised by the way it began. "Well," I say, "I lost my job." That's what initially sparked the fire that led me to start my company, Sales Acceleration Group, in 2016, after working for other people and companies for over twenty years.

"But," I'm quick to add, "I lead a blessed life. My story isn't the typical struggle story you hear from most small business owners." That always earns me a quizzical look. Because who reaches success without struggle, right?

I'm blessed but not because I'm "just lucky." Not only did I have the head start of learning sales and entrepreneurship from my family, but I also learned a very important principle. I call it "Do the right thing," and it's a "Kristieism" my clients hear quite often. But it comes down to making a practice of doing the right thing at the right time at every opportunity. My parents modeled it; my father's brother, my Uncle Bill, modeled it, and by the time I was old enough to make my own choices in my career and business, it was second nature for me. You'll learn more about this Kristieism, my parents, Uncle Bill, and all the times this principle has served me well, but just know that one reason I'm so blessed is that I've been doing the right things and helping the right people for a while now. My motto is always: "Do the right things; the right things will happen." And it's true.

Here's an example: for years, I've gone by the philosophy that I have thirty minutes for anyone, and people take me up on my offer. I regularly meet each week with people who are looking for a job and hope my network might be of help, or who need someone to review their resume, need career advice, need sales coaching, or need me to edit the "Dear John" breakup email to their boyfriend. I happily meet with those people because I believe helping people who don't know what I know, haven't had the opportunities I've had, or just need someone to tell them that they got this, is just the right thing to do.

So when I lost my job and needed a new one, I reached out to those people I'd had time for in the past and asked for their help. They stepped up in ways I never imagined. I was searching for an opportunity as a VP of Sales with a privately-owned Venture Capital (VC) backed SaaS (Software as a Service) company. As I met with people in my network, they began introducing me to people who they thought could help or who they knew would benefit from my skill set.

Then things took an unexpected turn. I can connect my current success back to one person, the owner of the first SaaS company I'd worked for, Dean Pichee. Our parting after ten years of working together wasn't as smooth as either of us wished it had been, but months after our parting, we got together for a beer and put our relationship back together because it was the right thing to do.

When I reached out to him after I lost my job and asked to grab lunch, he said he'd be happy to. I shared my situation with him and outlined the opportunity I was searching for. He said he'd introduce me to two people he thought I should meet. Those introductions were the first two dominos that started a chain reaction I could not have seen coming.

The first introduction he made was to a general partner of the largest VC firm in Missouri, John True. We met for breakfast, and I shared with him my desire to stay in the SaaS startup space and asked if he would keep his eyes open for me. He seemed like a nice man and said he would give some thought to who might benefit from my expertise. I had no expectations other than to have added a new person to my network. There was no way to know the impact this man would have on me personally and professionally as we parted ways that day.

The second introduction from Dean was to a husband-and-wife team who owned a SaaS software company. They were looking for a VP of Sales. We began the "courting" process of getting to know each other, and I was in the throes of interviewing with them when I received a call from John True. He asked me if I'd be willing to meet with the founder of a cybersecurity SaaS company they had funded who was ready to build out a sales team and looking for some advice. "Of course!" I said. It was the right thing to do.

I met with the founder for two hours and filled his notebook with advice and best practices about building a sales team from the ground up. At the end of our time together, he looked up and said how grateful he was that I shared all that amazing information with him. He then said, "There is no way I'm capable of doing all the things you just told me need to be done. Who do you know that can help me?" Before I stopped to think, I said, "I can!"

That company became my first client.

As I was pondering what I was going to do about the husband-and-wife team and their VP of Sales opportunity, which had looked so perfect only days before, I received a call out of the blue from a man I had met years earlier while working for Dean. This guy, David Freidman, ran a SaaS e-learning company in town that had been one of our channel partners so I had developed a relationship with him over the ten years I had worked for Dean's company.

He asked if we could meet for lunch. "Of course," I said. "I have thirty minutes for everyone!"

We spent the first fifteen minutes catching up about the last five years we hadn't been in touch, then I finally asked him, "So what did you really want to meet about?" He said the business had been struggling for the past couple of years, and he thought I might be able to offer some insight. "Sure," I said, "I'd be happy to look under the hood and see what might be amiss." He asked if I really had time to take on this project since I was working full-time. That's when I shared with him my situation, explaining that he'd asked at just the right time for me to welcome the distraction.

"Interesting," he said.

I met with him and his accounting person a few days later and quickly found a few impactful issues that were keeping his business from growing and his profit margin lower than it needed to be. After we reviewed the punch list of next actions to take, he said to me, "Would you be willing to spend an afternoon providing the sales team with sales training—paid, of course?"

"Absolutely!" I responded.

A week later, I delivered four hours' worth of sales training to his sales team. After that, he asked if I would do the same for his Customer Success team. You know my answer.

Two days after I finished delivering the training to the Customer Success team, he called me and said, "This is what you're supposed to be doing. You need to be helping owners and training sales teams, and I want to help you do that."

"What do you have in mind?" I asked.

"I want to help you build your business, and I want to be a client. I want you to lead my sales team fractionally. I want a minimum of ten hours of your time a week, but as you're building your business, I'll take up to thirty hours a week of your time and pay you accordingly until you get more clients. This is what you should be doing, and I want to help you get started."

They say you can't see the picture when you're inside the frame. And it's true. It's why even great sales leaders hire someone like me to show them their blind spots and why this man was able to look at what I was doing, how I was doing it, and how I came alive while I was doing it and see what I'd been missing for twenty years. This was exactly what I was meant to do.

When I say I've had a blessed life, I'm not kidding. David was stepping up to back a business I hadn't even dreamed of starting and didn't have any intention of building, and he was willing to underwrite me with hours and income until I was financially on my feet. He was essentially my business sugar daddy. I was nearly speechless (and when you get to know me, you'll understand just how rare an occurrence that is!). No one had ever been so generous or believed in me like that. Grateful is too small a word for how I felt, but I think that's the word I used when I said, "Yes!"

So that's how I got my second client and a legit business enterprise. After I wrapped my head around the fact that I was an entrepreneur, that I wasn't going to take a full-time, W2 employee, VP of Sales position, the excitement, fear, and imposter syndrome really hit me. I had repeatedly said for years that I had no interest in owning my own company. What was I thinking?

As I was setting up an LLC and trying to figure out what to call this new company, it occurred to me that I needed to let the husband-and-wife team know that I was no longer a candidate. Then it hit me. They had two account executives and one SDR (sales development representative). They didn't need a fulltime VP of Sales. They needed a fractional sales leader!

I set up a meeting with them and shared all the crazy things that had happened over the past few days and that I was no longer interested in being a full-time VP of Sales for them and instead thought they should become client number three. They said they were happy for me, but that they were committed to having a sales leader full-time. I totally understood, and we wished each other luck.

A week later, the husband reached out and asked me if I would meet with a consultant whom they had been working with. "Sure," I said. "Who's the consultant?"

"Mike Weinberg," he responded.

What? You're kidding, right? The guy who wrote *New Sales. Simplified*, the book I'd been using as training for the sales teams I'd been managing over the past few years? *That* Mike Weinberg?

Mike and I met over breakfast a few days later and, as he says, "We're siblings from another mother." We hit it off right away, and I told him about all the crazy, wonderful things that had been happening and the two clients I'd already secured. He said he thought I was perfect for this company and could help them. I reminded him that I'd already approached them about being a client, and they had turned me down because they were set on a full-time hire.

"Leave it to me," he said. "I'll make this happen."

True to his word, I got a call from the husband a day later asking me to come into the office to hammer out the details.

Not only did Mike help me secure my third client, but he also mentored me throughout my first year in business, and I'm eternally grateful to this day for his kindness, generosity, and confidence in me when I didn't have it in myself.

But the bottom line is that Sales Acceleration Group wouldn't exist today if it weren't for Dean Pichee. Dean took a chance on me in 2000 after I decided to leave the retail industry, and twenty-plus years later is still having an impact on my life. More to the point, my career in sales wouldn't be what it is if I hadn't been willing to start where I was and take the steps to "do the right thing," which actually took me exactly to where I really wanted to be.

Lessons to Sell By

I want to share just three of the lessons I've learned that account for me being in a position to write this book and will greatly contribute to *you* being where you want to be once you've read it and applied the principles, strategies, and tactics I've included. These are unpacked in detail in the following chapters but make note of them now, as they will be the foundation your strategy to sell your way in is built on.

Lesson One: Your circle matters.

Bring the smartest successful people with the highest character into your life and release back into the wild anyone whose time in your life has passed, or who does not actively support your journey.

Lesson Two: Do the right things, and the right things will happen.

Make time to mentor those who would benefit from your wisdom. Answer the call you think you're too busy to take, and if you think to yourself someone looks really good today, tell them. You don't know what people are going through and what impact it might have if you offer a kind word or gesture.

Lesson Three: When the Universe speaks, listen.

As a result of my parents owning a company for most of my life, I got to see firsthand the mental, emotional, physical, and financial toll owning a business can take. So I hadn't been shy about telling the Universe, and anyone else who would listen, that I had *absolutely* no desire to own my own company. But I couldn't deny there was something much bigger going on and that ignoring all the signs felt like a big mistake. Too many people and opportunities were converging all at once, and I knew something amazing was about to happen.

I'll never forget my dad telling me after a couple of years in business that being a consultant was the perfect job for me. "You get to speak your mind and tell people what they need to hear but don't want to hear, and instead of firing you, they'll actually pay you," he said.

He was right. I can't imagine doing anything else.

On your path to selling your way *in* to the life you want to live, you're going to get some of those signs from the Universe as well. Don't let your old way of thinking close your eyes and ears to the clues the Universe is sending your way.

What Does Selling Your Way IN Really Mean?

 There are jobs with a set income, and jobs where you set your income. You get to choose.

There's an expression for when a company is in a financial crisis, that there are only two choices: cut costs or "sell your way out of it." But mastering your ability to sell isn't about getting out of a crisis, or avoiding what you don't want. I don't teach people how to sell their way out so much as I help people use a career in sales to open doors and sell their way *in*, the same way I saw my parents use sales to open the doors to the life they wanted for themselves and my brother and me.

Those who know my family's story and how I got my MBA at the kitchen table often remind me that the business education I received growing up was extremely unusual, and as a result, I truly had a leg up in life. My front-row seat to seeing how our family went from a combined family income as a mid-level manager and teacher and seeing how our lifestyle changed as a result of running the number one real estate company in town, led by one of the top five agents in town, helped me understand that hard work does pay off, *and* if you pick the right profession, it can pay off in a *big* way.

Growing up in a sales family gave me a front row seat into the ups and downs of making a living selling and running a small business, so no one was more surprised than me when I decided to start my own business seven years ago. Neither my brother nor I ever discussed taking over the real estate company when our dad retired. I didn't even give that idea any consideration, and I don't think my brother did either. We had seen firsthand how hard it was to be a 100 percent commissioned real estate agent and a business owner, and yet, years later, we each chose similar sales roles as the ones our parents had chosen. My brother Scott makes the majority of his income from the commissions he earns, and I'm running my own company, solely dependent on my efforts for my livelihood. We've both come to understand that the financial pros of being in sales outweigh the cons of occasional stress and of starting every month at zero.

I don't believe that money buys happiness. But I know that it buys opportunities, and my life is proof of that. When I was thirty years old, I made what seemed like a rash decision at the time, to leave a retail career with a fortune 500 company, a profession where I'd built considerable success and a solid reputation, to enter the world of software sales. I'm grateful for all the opportunities my family and I have taken advantage of because of my decision to dedicate my professional life to a career in sales and sales leadership.

We often speak in sales about selling to your ICP (ideal customer profile), and true to form, I have an IRP (ideal reader profile). I want readers who love learning new things, who understand that your self-talk can propel you to success or limit your possibilities, who are willing to take risks to reap the rewards, and who know they have more to give and more to achieve and are willing to do the work to get there. If you fit that profile, then let's get started teaching you how to sell your way into a better life!

I want to start our journey together by making sure you really understand who you are. If you're not able to truly understand your strengths, what you like and what you don't, and what makes you uncomfortable, you could pick the wrong sales role, and picking the wrong sales role will impact your ability to be the best sales rep you can be and ultimately your income. So I'll ask you to get really honest with yourself so I can be of more help to you.

I'll then walk you through how to evaluate the different types of sales roles that are available and guide you in deciding what type of role will best play to your strengths, skills, and personality so that you will have an easy path to President's Club, beating the competition, or winning the big deal.

I want you to understand what your superpowers and secret weapons are, how to hone them, and when to use them to accelerate your career. You don't need to be great at everything. You just need to understand what special skills you have that differentiate you from the other 90 percent of sales reps.

I want to share my "three-year rule" and how putting that rule in play will make it so much easier for you to find the right prospects and close deals more quickly. I want you to understand that sales is part art and part science and how having a repeatable and customized process you can rely on is one of the keys to long-term success.

I want to teach you some sales shortcuts that, if you follow them consistently, will reduce the number of years it will take you to reach the top of your profession in the sales field of your choosing. I've worked with hundreds of sales reps and sales leaders over more than twenty years and seen what the Top 10 Percent are doing differently than the other 90 percent. I want to share their "secrets" with you so you can join them and live the life they are living.

Those are just a few of the areas we'll cover together as you make your way through the book. I know you think that you're reading a sales book, but I hope you'll realize this book is so much more. I've been blessed to have so many amazing people come into my life who've taught me so much about not only sales and business but about life. I couldn't have possibly written this book without all their wisdom being woven throughout. Wisdom I want to share with you so you'll not only be a better "person who sells" but also a better person who is happy and fulfilled in your chosen career.

I can't wait to hear from you after you've read the book about the changes you've made, the successes you've had, and the ways you're helping others who want to excel at sales do just that.

#Kristieisms: The Principles I Live By

Throughout this book you'll find a collection of hashtags, quips, mantras, and truisms that form the backbone of the principles I live by as a sales professional and person. My clients call them #Kristieisms, and I've summed up a number of them here for a quick and easy reference.

#ownyourownincome

I started the last section with the long form of this Kristieism: "There are jobs with a set income and jobs where you set your income. You get to choose." Well, this is the shortcut for that. It's a reminder that, in sales, you can always own your outcomes in order to own your income.

#ownyourownshit

This is a prerequisite for owning your own income, and you're going to see this one a lot! This was a result of the fatigue I was feeling every time a sales rep came into my office to complain about their territory, the marketing department, the product, their SDR (sales development representative), or even me! The more I've coached from this perspective, the more passionate about accountability I've become.

Before I recognized the power of personal accountability, I tried to be sympathetic about their rough life or personal circumstances, but when I did that, these sessions became a bitchfest and not solution-focused.

So I flipped the script and took the monkey off my back and put it on theirs. I would allow them to complain for a few minutes before I said, "Own your own shit." Their eyes always got big, and they just stared at me. Now that I had their attention, I said, "That's the issue; now what can you control? You can only control your behavior, so what do you want to do about what you can control?"

It's empowering to take control of a situation you initially believe is out of your control. So, #ownyourownshit.

 ## Process before Prospects

Clients often ask me to help them when they're ready to hire their first few sales reps. The first thing I ask is about formal and documented sales processes—as in, are there any? Engaging prospects before you've spent time to create, document, and hopefully test-drive your sales process is setting you up for failure. Make sure you have been trained on your company's process (or use the ones that have worked for you in the past) before reaching out to prospective clients.

 ## Move 'em forward or move 'em out, or #stalledisnotastage

I don't do "maybe." Either prospects, deals, or customers are making forward progress toward an end, or you need to consider moving them out of your line of sight. "Stalled" is not a stage in the sales cycle; if it's not moving, mark the deal as lost, move them out of your pipeline, assign them to an automated nurturing campaign, and set a reminder to call them in a few months when timing might be better. Letting people and deals sit idle for too long is a distraction and will become a source of frustration. Be in control of your sales process by having a walkaway point for people and deals that aren't moving forward.

Some money is better than no money

I'm not a big believer in discounting. You'll have to live with those discounts for the life of the customer. I'm also not a fan of losing a deal over price late in the game. I encourage reps to find a way to make a deal work, and if that means less money, there are ways to do that and maintain your credibility and integrity. It's okay to reduce the price in certain circumstances, as long as there are reduced features, functionality, or services. If you have a prospect with a problem you can solve who wants your company's help in solving that issue, think outside the box to put a deal together that can be the building blocks of a long-term relationship.

 ## Hunters aren't helpers

When I see reps that I've been told are hunters volunteering for every committee the company has and are willing to take on projects for the team, I know that I probably don't have a true hunter on my hands but most likely a farmer. Hunters are driven, focused, and have a desire to make sacrifices to achieve things they know others can't. The only thing a hunter is likely to volunteer for is helping pick the resort for the President's Club trip!

 ## Farmers want to raise the baby

When I explain the difference between hunters and farmers, I use this analogy: Hunters don't mind giving birth to the baby but have no interest in raising it. Farmers, on the other hand, would prefer to avoid the nine months of discomfort and the act of giving birth but couldn't imagine not watching the child take their first steps, walk into school on their first day of kindergarten, and walk the kid down the aisle. Farmers are all about the relationship and being there day in and day out to ensure their customers are successful.

"A-Player" privilege

As a sales leader in my twenties and early thirties, I thought all employees should be treated the same, in the interest of fairness. As I got older, I realized that not all employees perform the same, add the same value to the company, or have the same work ethic. As a result, I determined that top performers *should* have more flexibility and freedom. I call this "A-Player" privilege. "A-Players" are generally able to work more flexible schedules, work from home, and be allowed the ability to negotiate deals that involve price, terms, and other concessions.

Top performers build top-performer habits

You've heard the old adage, "It takes thirty days to make a habit." That's crap. It takes discipline! Top performers have developed habits that are now just like muscle memory for an athlete—automatic.

Titles are cheap, and business cards are cheaper

From time to time, I have an employee approach me who is not happy with the title they were given when they started. "No worries," I tell them. "What would you like your title to be?" I'm almost always willing to give someone a new title if it's important to them because new business cards are cheap. I'm not a big title person, but there are some performers whose identity is tied to their title. And there are some instances when a title brings enough credibility to make a difference to the prospect and move a deal along. If a new title will make someone happy or give them more confidence or industry cred, I'm all for it. Just remember that if I feel this way, other leaders might too, so don't judge a book by its title!

Help those who want to help themselves

I've been leading, training, and coaching employees since the day I got out of college, and the one thing I've learned is no matter how much wisdom I can impart or skills I can help them build, if they aren't interested in bettering themselves, then I'm wasting my time. So I prefer to spend my time with those who are committed to bettering themselves personally and professionally.

 ## If you want to earn at the top of the game, you have to play at the top of the game

Top 10 Percenters work the mental, physical, and spiritual game. They understand the work to get to the top doesn't happen at work; it happens outside of work. They also understand being the best requires discipline. That's why most don't get to the top.

 ## Panic causes bad decisions

When people are under stress, they are less likely to make sound and rational decisions. As it relates to sales reps, the biggest area that causes panic, and thus bad decisions, is not having enough deals in their pipeline to hit quota. The panic around anemic pipelines can cause reps to push a prospect harder than they should to close the deal sooner than the prospect is comfortable with, agree to a discount, or make other concessions, all because they don't have enough deals in their pipeline, and they need *this* deal to close because they don't have three or more they can choose from.

 ## Discovery isn't an event; it's a process

You hear sales pros talk all the time about having a discovery call. There are even sales stages that have the name, like "Stage 1: Discovery," but the truth is discovery isn't a one-time event or call; it's a process. Each time you meet with a prospect or customer you should be uncovering new information that you don't already know. The discovery process never ends.

 The data don't lie

Sales is part art and part science. Make sure you are making data-driven decisions, which means you'll need to have the data at your fingertips. The easiest way to do this is to have a personal dashboard in your CRM (Customer Relationship Management) system that helps you hone your craft and skills.

 Decisions are free; consequences are not

As my son got older and I could have more adult conversations with him, I regularly cautioned him that every decision he made would have consequences, which could have positive or negative results, so he needed to be thoughtful about those decisions. This is true for everyone, not just my son. When reps come to me and want to get outside the box (which I'm not opposed to), I make sure they understand what the consequences of doing so might be. Big and small decisions have consequences, so be thoughtful.

 I can't motivate the unmotivated, but I can inspire the self-motivated

I used to think it was my job to motivate my reps to do more, want more, and be more. I'd get frustrated and think I was a bad manager when I worked hard to motivate a rep, and no behavioral change happened. I put a lot of energy into figuring out why there were some people I couldn't seem to motivate. Over time, I noticed that all those people had one thing in common—they weren't self-motivated. I soon realized there wasn't anything I could do to change that. So I started spending my time with those who were self-motivated and focused on inspiring them to be their best selves. The results were rewarding for both of us.

 ## Do the right things, and the right things will happen

I truly believe that most people know the difference between right and wrong. I also believe that if everyone did what they knew to be the right thing, the world would be a better and kinder place. As it relates to sales, I believe doing the right thing is being honest with prospects about your product's or service's ability to really solve the issues they are facing and letting them know upfront if you don't believe your product or service is a fit for them based on budget, feature set, or even their culture.

 ## People are patterns

People are creatures of habit, so pay close attention to any behaviors that repeat themselves. I play singles tennis in a league. There aren't as many singles players as doubles players, so I end up playing the same people a few times each year. After every match, I go to my phone and pull up my tennis app, where I keep notes on every player I play. I record our scores and notes on the match, and I pay special attention to patterns I notice throughout the match and make note of those. I add information like, "She runs around her backhand," "When in trouble, she'll throw up a lob," or "80 percent of her forehands go down the line." I then use this valuable information the next time I face that opponent and enjoy watching her scratch her head when I'm right where I'm supposed to be on the court when she takes her forehand down the line.

Success in sales is as much about observation and psychology as strategy and tactics. Pay attention and take note when prospects and customers react the same way in similar situations each time. It's much easier for you to prepare for what's coming when you can anticipate it and plan ahead. Look for times when they are uncomfortable, react defensively, or react positively—what's being discussed? The best defense is a good offense.

The best predictor of future behavior is past behavior

This one is closely related to "People are Patterns." The reason I ask behavioral-based interview questions is because the way a person dealt with a certain situation in the past is a good indicator of how they will deal with similar situations in the future. I also take this concept and use it to help me predict how a prospect will act during the sales cycle. I ask questions such as these to help me foresee the future:

1. How do you normally go about getting approval for these types of purchases?
2. What questions does your boss normally ask before deciding to support a purchase such as this?
3. What have you done in the past to ensure a successful implementation?
4. How do you determine which vendor to go with when multiple vendors are in the running?

Use the past to predict the future, and you'll have people suspecting that you might just own a crystal ball.

 It has to be all about them before it can be all about you, and before it can be all about us

It's just a truth when you're dealing with humans. You *must* put the prospect and customer's needs before your own. They have to believe that you care about helping them solve their issues and improve their situation before they will be willing to listen to you talk about your service and company or consider you a partner. This is why a great discovery process is so important.

If you don't choose your clients, they will choose you!

Sales pros love to complain about not getting inbound leads from marketing, but the truth is those inbound leads aren't usually prospects you want to sell to. The only way to pick your clients is to proactively go after them through outbound efforts, trade shows, or referrals and networking.

 You can't fix character flaws, integrity issues, or what mama broke

This one might feel harsh, but it's given me the ability to just trust my intuition and live with the fact that I can't make everyone successful. I can't take credit for this Kristieism, though. The credit goes to a former boss who said this to me one day when we were discussing a candidate, and our guts told us something was off about them. We just couldn't put our finger on what it was that made us shy away from hiring them. Finally, my boss said, "You can't fix character flaws, integrity issues, or what mama broke. It's just one of those things; let's pass on the candidate." I use this #kristieism anytime something feels off, and I can't quite put my finger on it.

 **#SowtoGrow**

You must have a growth mindset. When I interview candidates for a sales position, one of the characteristics I'm looking for is a commitment to continuous learning. Someone who understands that unless they invest in themselves professionally and personally, they can't reach the highest level in their career. I call it "Sow to Grow." You need to understand that you can't reach your full potential unless you invest in yourself each and every day. I ask candidates what the last book was they read, what podcasts do they listen to, and who they follow on social media. You must always be planting seeds to have a fruitful harvest.

These are just some of the principles I live and sell by and say often enough that I've become known for them. But I want to make sure you're clear about the difference between principles and values. Principles are rules that you live by and that influence your behavior. Values are what is important to you and actually guide you in developing your principles. I'm a "rules girl," so it's no surprise that I've developed a number of principles over the years. I'm all about making my life easier, and for me, that includes having a set of rules I can fall back on to make an automatic decision, just like an athlete uses muscle memory to react the same way in similar situations.

I would encourage you to use your personal values to create your own set of guiding principles, that you can use to make good decisions in every moment.

SECTION ONE

DEVELOPING YOUR PERSONAL PLAN FOR BECOMING A ROCK STAR PROFESSIONAL

The one thing that leads to the greatest failure rate in sales isn't a lack of training, skill, or even discipline. It's a lack of self-awareness. People who don't know themselves inevitably make poor career decisions. They allow themselves to be put in positions and situations that run counter to their nature or that aren't fulfilling. They don't know how to leverage their strengths or overcome their weaknesses. They won't grow and develop as humans, let alone as sales professionals.

Self-awareness is also important to creating credibility and trust, two essential characteristics in sales. In fact, show me a salesperson who doesn't know themselves, and I'll show you a salesperson who doesn't trust themselves and won't be able to earn the trust of their prospects because of it.

So let's start with getting to know the most important person to your sales success—you.

1

You've Got to Meet Yourself
Before You Meet the Prospect

I t's been a long time since I worked for tips, and I've had a lot of great career experiences since then, but still today, my favorite job was waiting tables. Not only did it teach me many of the lessons and skills I've used to build my sales career, but it also taught me something even more important—it taught me about myself.

In sales, you're going to hear a lot about knowing your prospect, knowing your market and industry, knowing your product, and knowing the company and the team you work with. In fact, we're going to talk a lot about all of that in Section Two. But none of that will mean anything if you don't know yourself. And I don't just mean your strengths and weaknesses or your personality traits. I mean knowing what drives you, how you like to be rewarded, and what kicks your butt and takes the wind out of your sails every time.

Sales can be exciting, even exhilarating. But it can also be demanding, daunting, even dehumanizing. If you know what fires you up, and you're in a position that delivers that on the regular, you'll be able to draw on that energy to keep you in the game on days that might otherwise be irredeemable.

I started my waitressing "career" at a family restaurant/ice cream parlor while I was still in high school. I worked mostly nights and weekends during the school year and added on days in the summer. This was my starter job. It was waiting tables where I first learned about myself and what I really needed to be fulfilled in my work, and I've leveraged that self-knowledge to tailor everything from job opportunities, sales strategies and processes, and a business model for the business I now run.

The first thing I realized about why I loved waiting tables was that I received feedback on my performance in real time. Once a table cleared, I could walk over to pick up my tip and basically get a scorecard as clearly as if there were judges holding up signs with numbers on them. I wanted all tens, but it was the instant feedback in the form of my tip that motivated me.

After each shift, I'd head home and sit down on the floor in the family room. I'd take out my Space Sak pouch where I kept each night's haul and dump it all out on the floor to count it up. Dad was almost always there watching TV, and I'd share the total with him so he could rate the night's take.

I competed with myself each shift to see if I could make more money than the previous shift. The "sport" of waiting tables was perfect for me—fast-paced, personality-packed, and profitable! While my friends were working minimum wage jobs, I was bringing in twice as much money with enough time on my hands to work on my tan lines in the summer.

That love of "wins," of competing with myself, as well as thriving on the pace and pressure, loving the human interaction, and being motivated by the ability to own my own income (#ownmyownincome) is just inherently who I am. And I soon leveraged it into an even more successful opportunity.

I left that position after about a year and moved up to a nicer restaurant that sold beer and wine along with a higher quality of food. I wasn't working any harder, but my tips were about 35 percent higher each shift.

By the time I got into college, I had figured out the concept of working smarter, so I took a job waiting tables at a restaurant with a sports bar in the basement. One shift at the restaurant on a weekend night could net me between $75 to $100. Then, unexpectedly, I got my big break. One Saturday night, the manager approached me and said that one of the cocktail waitresses at the sports bar had called in sick, and he needed me to fill in. Never one to turn down an opportunity to make money while watching sports, I was all in! I felt very grown up as I headed to the basement since I wasn't even old enough to drink any of the beverages I would be serving.

The bar was a dark, loud, testosterone-heavy den. The pace was ridiculous, and I quickly found out that balancing a tray full of drinks while navigating your way through a rowdy crowd cheering for the home team was not for the faint of heart. By the end of the six-hour shift, I was exhausted, but my apron was heavy, and I couldn't wait to get home, dump that night's take on the floor, and count it up. I made over $200 that night. "So," I said to myself, "this is what it's like to play in the big leagues!" I was shocked. And I was hooked.

There are so many similarities between waiting tables and sales. Just like sales, *what* you sell matters. I quickly learned that when I worked nights in a nice restaurant that sold alcohol, my average check, and thus my tip, was bigger. Much bigger. Second, territory matters. The section I was assigned each shift could mean a difference of $40 in tips. Third, relationships with your coworkers matter. Getting a "good" section was up to the managers, so guess who I buttered up to (pun intended). Fourth, the way you take care of your clients matters. A lot! I had regulars, people who would ask to be seated in my section because I took good care of them, and they took care of me financially. And fifth, product knowledge matters. What were the night's specials, how was a dish prepared, did the salad have nuts in it? It all matters to the clients, and it all mattered to my tip total too!

While all those things transferred to a career in sales, the most important lesson I learned during my six years of waiting tables was that there are jobs where you have a set income and jobs where you set your income. You have a choice! And a job where I got to set my income was, without a doubt, my choice.

I *definitely* learned that I preferred to set my income without being dependent on an employer to acknowledge the quality of my work, without waiting for a performance review and a 3 percent raise, and without worrying about budget cuts or salary freezes. A set income limits me; a career in sales puts me in control of my income and my destiny.

Waiting tables taught me that one of the ways I like to be rewarded is with money and the ability to control how much I make, but it was my love of racquetball that taught me another way that I get to feel rewarded for my work—in the joy of helping others succeed.

I started playing racquetball when I was fourteen. By the time I was sixteen, I was traveling around the four-state area, playing tournaments several weekends a year. It suited my love of fierce competition, challenging my athletic abilities, and it took care of the calories that are an occupational hazard of working in the restaurant business.

When I got to college, I went in search of a job with flexible hours I could work during the week and that worked with my class schedule. I figured this way, if I couldn't wait tables on the weekends because of a tournament, I'd at least have a little bit of money coming in. I decided to talk to the owner of the only racquetball club in town. Why not combine my love of racquetball with my need for some extra income? Sure enough, I was able to pick up a few hours each week working the front desk. This was a win-win: a free membership, so I could practice anytime I wanted, and a little extra cash.

One day, a member of the club was watching me practice, and he yelled down from above, "Do you give lessons?"

"I don't," I said.

Then he yelled again, "Would you give lessons?"

"Sure," I said.

His name was Randy, and he wasn't a "natural" at racquetball, but he shared my mindset for what I call "sow to grow"—investing in yourself to get what you want. He was not only willing to pay me for lessons, but he was also willing to put in the hours and the effort to get better at the game.

I began giving Randy one or two lessons a week. I had no formal process or strategy for teaching him; I just took what I had learned from my coach, Pete, and shared it with Randy. Even though Randy paid me to give him lessons, I soon realized I would have done it for free (don't tell Randy). I loved seeing his excitement when he mastered a new skill or beat an opponent he'd never beaten before. I learned that I received a great deal of pleasure helping others improve their ability regardless of how much I was paid or whether I was paid anything at all. It gave me a thrill to see them take the help I offered and turn it into a success of their own.

Do you understand how you like to be rewarded for a job well done? Are you money motivated? Do you like to see your name at the top of the leaderboard? Is public recognition important to you? Or are you just happy knowing that you helped make your prospect's life easier?

It's important that you understand what your reward structure is so you can pick a sales role that fits your financial and emotional needs. Sales can be a risky profession. It's the reward you get that makes the risk worth it.

Of course, it's also important to understand your personality and preferences. They say your personality traits are formed at an early age, before ten, so you've probably got at least a decade of your own history to review. I want you to ask yourself this: what personality traits do you have that will not only help you decide the best type of sales job for you, but will also provide you the highest income so you can have the life you dream of? What preferences make some jobs or routines easier for you?

You know how I learned that waitressing at the sports bar was more fun and more profitable than the family restaurant? It worked for me because it suited my personality and preferences. For me it was no "harder" to wait tables in the sports bar than it was in the family restaurant. I loved sports, so it was actually more fun to wait on people who also loved sports in a place where every television was tuned to a game. And since my tips were usually higher in the sports bar, I'd say that qualified as working "smarter, not harder." But for someone who didn't enjoy the atmosphere of the sports bar, no amount of money was going to make the "smarter, not harder" way work.

The same will be true as you make decisions about how you're going to design your sales career. Take, for example, my experience with two successful sales reps, Tiffany and Matt. Tiffany was on what a lot of people might call the "work harder" program. She contacted more people and made more calls than any of her counterparts. Her strategy was to play the numbers game with really big numbers, and because she *preferred* the hustle of casting a wide net over and over.

Matt was the exact opposite. Where Tiffany probably made thirty calls a day, Matt may have only made thirty calls a week. His strategy was to do a lot of research, ensuring that he got the person in the company who he thought gave him the highest probability of engagement and an eventual closed sale. He went after bigger, more challenging deals, and he also loved selling onsite. This let him satisfy his need for a lot of variability and flexibility, which helped him to really enjoy the day-to-day of sales. For him, "working smarter" meant frontloading the work in research, showing up in person, and having the patience and tenacity to work a long sales cycle with a bigger payout at the end. At the end of the year, both Tiffany and Matt were over quota and had earned Rock Star status, and their self-awareness of what they were good at and enjoyed most was what led them to tailor their "smarter, not harder" strategy to their strengths.

You need to really know who you are and what you want before you'll be able to put yourself in a position to truly kick a$$ and be one of the Top 10 Percenters—a "Sales Rock Star." There are so many different sales opportunities to choose from, and I'm going to cover those later in this book. But if you don't truly know yourself, you're likely to pick the wrong sales role for you. And that could have long-lasting, negative effects. In the wrong sales job, you could end up thinking that you're not cut out for sales, you might lose your job, or you could hold yourself back from maximizing your income.

It's taken years for me to figure out who I am, what I'm passionate about, what I have to offer the world, and how to maximize my income.

Over time, I've taken what I learned at each position, considered what I liked and what I didn't, learned what I excelled at and what I struggled with, and then I applied that knowledge when deciding what I wanted my next opportunity to be.

Let me run you through a series of questions I use with people when I'm trying to help them determine what the best sales role would be for them.

Question One:

If you miss your flight and end up at the airport hotel for the night, are you more likely to belly up to the lobby bar to meet new people and make some new connections, or will you head straight to your room and order room service?

Although my son calls it being nosy, I've always preferred the term "naturally curious." I tell people that I can't teach natural curiosity or social boldness. So if I'm stuck in a hotel in a strange city with nothing else to do, you're going to find me at the lobby bar, and most likely, I'll know a fair amount about those sitting around me by the time last call comes around. Because my new bar friends are really strangers, whom I will most likely never see again, you can expect me to ruthlessly grill them. After all, I'm just there to entertain myself!

I believe curiosity and social boldness are traits that are either inherent or developed at a young age. I also believe they are critical for hunters. If you don't love learning about other people, aren't curious about other people's stories and situations, and aren't willing to take a chance to try to strike up a conversation, you won't love being a hunter and will have more success in another role, like farmer.

Questions Two and Three:

Tell me the hardest decision you've made in the last few years.

Tell me the last time a friend said to you, "I can't believe you just did that"; and what was the circumstance that led them to say that?

Both of those questions help me understand what I call your "risk profile." Understanding your risk profile will help you truly determine which job might be for you and which could become a demoralizing disaster. People with a high-risk profile are willing to start at zero every month, meaning you begin every month with no revenue on the board, which is what a hunter has to do. Hunters are more likely to love a job with an early-stage startup or starting a new division of their company. They are comfortable with failure but understand the biggest risks usually come with the biggest rewards and commission checks.

What role should you look for if you have a low-risk profile? You're more likely to love a position where you can have an ongoing relationship with a customer, such as an account manager or customer success rep. These positions will have a higher base-to-commission ratio and will focus on maintaining and growing a customer, instead of hunting to find them to begin with. You'll be building a relationship with a customer who has already made the hard decision to buy from your company. Now all you need to do is help them get value for their investment. If this is you, you're a farmer, not a hunter.

Questions Four and Five

Are you more likely to ask for forgiveness or permission? The follow-up question, regardless of the answer, is:

Can you give me an example of a time that strategy bit you in the butt?

I ask question four because it also gives me insight into whether the individual is a hunter or a farmer. Hunters will typically ask for forgiveness and farmers will ask for permission.

Question five lets me know how self-aware you are and how difficult you might be to manage. I'm all in for managing a Lone Wolf who is likely to believe that asking for permission is a waste of time and shouldn't ever bite them in the butt, but Lone Wolves aren't for everyone, and they aren't a fit in every organization.

Question Six:

What's the craziest thing you've ever done to close a sale?

I once had a candidate tell me they had a large deal they needed to close by the end of the month, but the prospect had become elusive. He'd stopped returning calls and emails, and the candidate was afraid that not closing this deal would put his monthly and quarterly quota in jeopardy.

So he headed to the office of the prospect and sat in the lobby all day until the prospect left at the end of the day. He called out to the prospect as he walked by and asked him if he could walk him to his car. Well, you already know how this story ends. Quota attained!

Being professionally persistent isn't comfortable for everyone, and that's why I ask the question. I'm trying to determine if you have a creative or no-fear attitude. This also helps me know a little about your desire to succeed. I need to determine how far out of your comfort zone you're willing to go to get the sale.

I often find candidates apply for jobs based on the title of the position and don't spend time really digging into the job description and requirements of the position. As a result, I often find farmers applying for hunter positions (the same isn't usually true in reverse).

When I'm helping a client hire a hunter, farmer, or gatherer (someone who is both hunter and farmer), every question I ask and every answer I get is helping me determine if the candidate's strengths tie to the needs of the position. I also need to determine if the candidate I'm speaking with is capable of not just doing the job but of becoming a Top 10 Percenter.

I know I'm not a typical interviewer. You may very well interview with dozens of sales managers or consultants that don't ask questions like these. But I'm not only looking to find the best candidate for my client, I also feel a sense of obligation to make sure the candidate is making the right decision and is an educated consumer. There are times when I interview a candidate who, from a skill perspective, is capable of being a hunter but from a desire and joy perspective, would rather be a farmer or a gatherer who, at a minimum, wants to keep the client after the sale and nurture and grow that account. I feel it's my responsibility, as someone with over twenty-five years of sales leadership experience, to help candidates understand themselves better and help them pick the correct position. There's a difference between those who can do the job and those who are passionate about the sales role. Those who are passionate will not only be happier but will also make more money.

You may never interview with me, but you can use these same questions to get more insight into your ideal fit in the sales arena. Take some time to think about your sales skill strengths and the past positions you've not only excelled at, but really enjoyed and felt fulfilled doing. I've included a quiz later on in the book to help you understand the best sales role for you.

All sales positions have pros and cons; the challenge is picking the position that will reward you financially and satisfy you emotionally. If you want to learn to "sell your way in" to a satisfying job or life situation, you must get to know yourself before you make that decision.

2

Recognizing and Leveraging Your Rock Star Sales Traits

There are a number of character traits that will serve you well in your sales career. Persistence, a strong work ethic, and accountability are three high on my list to look for. But if there is any trait that a Rock Star sales rep must have, it's confidence. And I don't mean the cocky, fast-talking, stereotypical car salesman arrogance. I mean the deep and often quiet confidence that unconsciously lets your prospect know they can trust you, that you're an expert in your field, that you've got their back, and that they've got nothing to worry about.

If you want to know the kind of confidence I mean, let me tell you about James. Back in 2005, I was leading a fast-growing SaaS sales team. James applied for an account executive position, and I loved him in the first interview. He was charismatic, articulate, personable, extroverted, and *definitely* confident. He had been successful at his last sales position over the past three years. He was just what I was looking for in an account executive, so I made him an offer, and he accepted.

During his first week, James came to me to ask if the company would purchase a software program called Dragon Naturally Speaking. I was unfamiliar with this product, so I asked him to explain what it was and why he needed it. He explained it was voice recognition software that would allow him to put his verbal notes into the written word. Once I understood what the software did, I asked him why he needed it. James explained that he was dyslexic. Note-taking was time-consuming and energy draining for him, and try as he might, he was still prone to spelling mistakes.

James told me that he used this software program to dictate his notes into the CRM system and other applications, which would not only save him time and prevent spelling mistakes he might otherwise make but would also leave him free to do more of what we hired him to do—sell.

I was shocked. I had no idea from the interview that James had overcome such a challenge to build the success he'd had in his sales career. It was at this point, after agreeing to purchase the software for him, that I asked exactly what challenges this had posed for him over the years. He told me he had been assigned a "proctor" in college to take notes for him in class and write out the answers to exam questions as he dictated them to her. That brought up the obvious question, "How have you managed to be so successful with such a challenging learning disability?"

"I learned to develop my interpersonal skills over the years," he said. "I used humor to distract my classmates from the fact I didn't always know the correct answer, and I used my personality to win over the teachers so they would go easier on me."

Impressive. Instead of feeling sorry for himself, he decided to play to his strengths. And the strengths he developed, out of necessity, were also the traits of a successful sales rep.

I would say that it was James' confidence that first got my attention, but at the end of the interview, I just really liked him, wanted to be around him, and had to have him on my team. James turned his adversity into a way to hone his ability to draw people in. He was just plain likable. He was a supremely competent and confident sales rep, and I still frequently use a quote James had in his email signature: "My second favorite word is no!"

Now that's confidence.

I want to veer a bit to the left for just a minute to discuss the difference between confidence and self-confidence. Confidence draws on prior experiences and successes from the past. As I've said, the best predictor of future behavior is past behavior. If you've sold $1M in the past, you'll have the confidence you can do it again. But if you're given a $1M quota for this year, and you've never sold $1M before, you'll need to rely on your self-confidence to get you there. Self-confidence comes from within: the ability to trust and believe in yourself and to know you can take the success you've had in one area of your life and apply those same principles and beliefs that created that success to other areas of your life. They aren't the same thing, but they're both traits you'll want to develop.

I remember sitting down with Mike Weinberg, Rock Star sales expert and best-selling author, as he challenged me to charge more for my consulting services when I was starting my consulting business. "But I've never done this before," I protested. "I can't charge as much as those who've been doing this for ten years."

"You *have* done this before," he reminded me. "You're a successful sales leader who brings twenty-plus years of hands-on experience to the table, and people will be willing to pay for that."

Confidence will take you places you can't go without it. The good news is that anyone can build the confidence they need to go the places they want to go. Mike helped me push my imposter syndrome aside. He was right. I had years of sales leadership experience and success helping companies, teams, and individual reps increase revenue and profit. I needed to pull from my prior successes to give me greater confidence *and* rely on the self-confidence I had developed from learning to believe and trust in myself.

Here are a few of the tips and tools I teach to continually build confidence:

Be aware of your body language. Are you inadvertently telegraphing to others that you lack confidence just based on how you carry yourself? Throw your shoulders back, look people in the eye, and use your command voice when you meet people in person. Even if you're not feeling super confident in the moment, you'll feel more confident and will portray that confidence to others.

Stop negative self-talk in its tracks. As I discussed earlier, I've been a competitive athlete my entire life. Because of a fair amount of self-awareness at an early age, I knew that I received only just enough natural athleticism from the parental gene pool, and I'd have to rely on other things to compete at a high level. One of the things I relied on was positive self-talk. I stopped negative self-talk as soon as it entered my head and replaced it with a phrase I still use to this day: "You're the winner." Not *a* winner, but *the* winner. The winner of this game, set, match.

Pull from past successes. I've been known to regularly say, "Success begets success." The best time to make a sale is right after you've made a sale. I often tell reps who've just brought in a deal to pick up the phone and call the prospect you expect to close next and see if you can make it rain a second time in one day. Your confidence is at its highest right after you've had success, so use that confidence and momentum to extend your winning streak. I also tell reps who've had a kick-ass chart-topping month or quarter to put in writing all the things they believe they did that contributed to their success so they'll have those notes to pull from if they hit a slump or have a tough day.

Confidence is critical to Rock Star status, but it isn't the only trait you'll benefit from developing. When I think back over the twenty-five-plus years of leading sales reps, the Top 10 Percent all had some or all of the following traits in common:

Practice discipline.

There are no lazy Rock Stars. In the book *Outliers: The Story of Success* by Malcom Gladwell's research shows that the best in every field from basketball to real rock stars, like Mick Jagger, put in 10,000 hours of intense practice to reach mastery in their field. Ten thousand hours of practice requires incredible discipline. Prospecting, selling on value, not giving in to demands for discounts, and asking for referrals consistently require discipline.

Show your grit.

Angela Duckworth, author of the book *Grit,* defines grit as passion and perseverance for long-term goals. Sales is all about the long game. You need to stay the course to have long-term success.

Have a short memory.

Sales is a rejection-filled sport. Having short-term memory issues, in this case, is a good thing. If there's a lesson to be learned, make a note of it and move on to the next opportunity. Dwelling on the negative and what went wrong just won't benefit you in the long run.

Develop a dash of rebel.

Let's call this one optional but preferred. Those Top 10 Percenters were a little hard to manage from time to time, and I respected that about them. But they also kept me entertained and engaged, which is always a plus.

Bring your own pom-poms.

See "short memory" for the why. Some say mind over matter; I say the mind matters. Under the list of things you can control, this should be at the top of the list. You need to be your own cheerleader. Sales is hard, so be sure you celebrate every win, big and small.

Turn on the charisma.

Charisma is that special something you can't always put your finger on and is very closely tied to confidence. Sales reps with charisma draw people to them, are great listeners, exude tremendous confidence, and make people feel important. Charisma can be used for good or evil, so make sure you're using your charisma to build trust, not sell snake oil.

Practice realism.

My son uses the term "Dream Killer," but I prefer to consider myself a realist. I find the sales reps who can be objective are more likely to succeed. They can determine, without emotion, if a prospect really has a problem their product or service can solve, if they will be willing to spend money to solve that problem, and if they really have the authority to make a buying decision. You need to have this ability to see things the way they really are and not how you'd like them to be if you're in sales. It's a true superpower. Realism combined with discipline will **keep you from** 1. leaving stalled deals in your pipeline, 2. allowing prospects to continuously tell you maybe, and 3. letting your manager believe you're going to hit your quarterly quota when you aren't.

Develop resilience.

The ability to recover from disappointments or failures quickly is critical. The longer you dwell on the "what ifs," the longer it will take you to be productive, close your next deal, or take the next risk. Sales is full of opportunities to beat yourself up over. Resist the urge to do so. If there are lessons to be learned, acknowledge those and move on.

Practice self-care.

I consistently ask the following interview question: "Name three activities or tasks you do, regardless of the job you have, that you think have led to your success." Of the true 10 Percenters, most will mention exercise, meditation, clean eating, or a religious or spiritual practice. The mind-body connection is well-documented. Find something you can do to challenge your mind, body, or spirit every day to make you stronger and ready for the what life hands you.

Maintain integrity.

This goes back to "Do the right things, and the right things will happen." I'll give you an example: When I was VP of Business Development for a SaaS company, a prospect left me a voicemail, which was the first and last time that ever happened. I did a little research on him and his company before returning his call. When we spoke, he told me he was interested in figuring out if a product like ours could help them. I launched into discovery mode and asked a few questions to confirm my earlier research. After learning more, I told him I didn't believe he needed our product yet, due to the size of his team. I told him there were similar but cheaper options he should probably start with, and when the team grew to X number of employees, we should talk again.

A year or so later, after I'd left that company and had started my consulting business, he reached out to me on LinkedIn and wanted to talk. I had no memory of him or our conversation at my previous employer. When we connected on the phone, I told him as much and he started to refresh my memory about our conversation. I then remembered him and our conversation (I rarely had a prospect end up in my voicemail so that alone made it memorable), and I asked him why he reached out. He told me he saw that I was now consulting, and he was having issues with their sales team. He thought I could help.

"Wow," I said. "I'm surprised you remembered me and have been keeping up with my journey."

He replied, "I've never had anyone refuse to sell me something before. You made an impression."

I ended up spending a year helping them turn their sales team around, and he became one of my largest clients at that time. It was a perfect reminder to have integrity and always stay true to my values.

These traits can all be developed over time. Start with being honest with yourself about which traits you already own and which have just been renting space month to month. Traits like discipline, positivity, and not dwelling on disappointment and failure are traits that will be easier to learn and develop than say, charisma, but they can have just as great an impact on your ability to become a Top 10 Percenter.

3

Know Your Strengths

If there is any career where playing to your strengths is critical, it's sales. It's why the #sowtogrow mindset is so important for creating the ability to sell your way out of anything you don't want and *into* the life you really desire.

Our brains are wired for survival, so our default is to always be on the lookout for danger. It's no wonder we're experts at identifying the weaknesses and not the strengths in ourselves. This survival tendency is then rewarded and reinforced by pretty much everyone around us. We do postmortems (which literally means examining a dead body) after a project or deal goes south. Performance reviews tend to focus more on "opportunities for improvement" rather than what we did well. Leaders tend to, often unconsciously, catch employees doing something wrong instead of looking to catch them doing it right. So it's no wonder when we're asked about our strengths, we have to dig a little deeper to come up with them and then try not to feel like we're bragging when we share them out loud.

You can't be successful if you don't have awareness about your strengths, and you certainly can't play to your strengths if they're still shrouded in mystery. Sometimes, your strengths are obvious to you and others, and other times, they are hidden from you but obvious to others. What's important is that you uncover and understand what your sales strengths are so you can turn them into your sales superpower, which we'll cover later.

If you are fully aware of your strengths and what you do better than others, that's great. But if you aren't sure you have a handle on what your strengths are, here are a couple of suggestions to help you uncover that hidden treasure:

Think about what tasks seem to come easy to you. What do you enjoy doing? Ask those close to you what they think you do better than most. Maybe you're a good listener (very important in sales) or you have strong problem-solving skills (also very important, especially for farmers and gatherers). Survey your friends and family to see what they think.

Some of your personal strengths may be hard-won or developed through adversity the way James developed his charisma and confidence as a response to being dyslexic. Some strengths may have been learned through experience, and some may just be your natural gifts. No matter how your strengths came to be, you need to continue to develop and hone them to keep them sharp.

Remember how Mike helped me recognize my strengths? The best advice I give anyone is to pay attention when someone shows you strengths you didn't know you had. Especially if that someone is a few miles ahead of you on your path, or if they have expertise in your field. Let me share a story about how a hidden strength turned into an amazing opportunity for Brent, a colleague of mine.

I have a pretty good "radar" for the kinds of strengths that make someone really good in a sales role. But sometimes, I have to give them time to recognize and acknowledge their own strengths. Then I can help them to cash in on those strengths. Brent is a great example of someone who had to fully own his strengths before he could find success in sales.

I met Brent in 2014 when I joined a Venture Capital-backed SaaS startup as the director of Business Development. Brent was a project manager there and worked closely with the development team. I took to Brent right away. He was outgoing, super funny, and extremely articulate. As I got to know him better, my instincts told me he'd make a great sales rep. I started to talk to him about coming to "the dark side."

He resisted my recruiting advances and said he was happy where he was. Furthermore, he thought selling was hard and stressful. Imagine that! I touted the glories of being a sales rep: the challenge, the thrill of victory, and of course, the money. He turned me down cold.

But it turned out that Brent had actually been listening when I pointed out the strengths that made me believe he'd be good in sales. Not long after, he tracked me down and said the company had approached him about being its first solution consultant. An SC is someone who is part of the sales team and responsible for demoing the software to prospects, so it isn't necessary for the sales rep to be a technical expert to close deals. He asked me what I thought of the idea. I loved it and told him so.

"This is the best of all worlds," I said. "You get to have an impact on sales, you'll get a commission on deals you're involved in that close, *and* you don't have a quota to stress you out. It's perfect."

Brent started as a solution consultant in 2015. He was promoted to manager of solution consultants in 2018, then to director in 2019, and today, he is the VP of Solution and Value Consulting.

He didn't initially see what I saw, but he was willing to listen even if he wasn't ready to jump into sales with both feet. And I clearly wasn't the only one who thought he had sales in his DNA. He said my persistence (I think he really meant harassment) in telling him he had the right strengths for the role made him more open to the idea of being a solution consultant when the company approached him. It really was his gift, and this particular position was a great fit for him and allowed him to play to his strengths. It was a win for him and a win for the company.

4

Play to Your Strengths

dentifying your strengths (or having someone else point them out as I did in Brent's case) will allow you to move on to the next step—playing to your strengths. This is what helps us perform at our best and excites and energizes us, which will bring us more joy and less stress and help us find meaning and purpose in our work. All of this will lead to fulfillment and prosperity.

So the good news is work can feel like play, and play can include work *if* your current sales role allows you to play to your strengths. But what if that isn't the case? What if your current sales role doesn't allow you to play to your strengths? Now what? Honestly, it's time to make what I call a "step-change." A step-change is when you leave your current position (but not necessarily your company) and take the next "right" step that will get you further down the career path and closer to your end goal. This could be a more challenging position, a position with more financial opportunities, or a slight left turn, like Brent made, that will move you in the right direction.

To play to your strengths, you must be in the correct sales role. As we'll discuss in the next chapter, there are as many sales roles as there are flavors of ice cream, so the goal is to find the right position that will allow you to play to your strengths.

Let me share an example from my childhood. I was an active child (that might be an understatement), and when I was around five, the neighbor up the street asked my parents if I might like to play T-ball over the summer on the team she coached. My parents thought that anything that helped me burn some energy was a good thing, so they signed me up.

I loved the sport. It combined three of my favorite things: team, outdoors, and competition, and over the thirteen years I played softball, I identified a few strengths. I learned that I had great eye-hand coordination, a strong arm, no fear of the ball or of the damage it could do, and although I wasn't a fast runner, I was quick—stealing bases was my thing, and I have a scar on my left knee to prove it.

Over the years, I played a few positions. I started at first base, but that really didn't play to my strong arm, so the coach moved me to third base where we would have a better chance of throwing out a runner at first base on a ground ball to third. I liked playing third base since it played to more of my strengths—my strong arm, my lack of fear of the ball, and my quickness.

At some point, Coach decided that my strong arm and quickness could be put to better use, and I was moved to left field. Although I didn't feel as connected to what was going on in the infield, there was nothing like the feeling of catching a fly ball and then watching the runner on third tag and make their way toward home plate, only to be shocked when I fired the ball to my catcher, and they were stopped short of scoring. Double plays were my favorite, of course.

Around the time I entered high school, a similar situation to my big waitressing break happened. Our catcher got hurt during the game, and Coach said he needed someone to volunteer to catch. The reaction from the team was about the same as when the public speaking teacher asks for a volunteer to stand up in front of the class and give their speech first. Eyes averted and backs turned. Although softball was a bit of a dirty sport, there was still makeup involved, and catching was . . . well, not glamorous.

The gear, the mask, squatting down with the umpire breathing on your neck—you get the picture. After just enough awkward silence had passed, I raised my hand and said I'd do it.

It took two of us to get the gear on me, and then I felt like the Tin Man from *The Wizard of Oz* as I awkwardly walked behind home plate. I squatted down, and the umpire gently suggested I scoot back so as to not get my hand taken off by the opponent swinging the bat. After I was safely out of the range of the bat, I looked at my pitcher and signaled that I was ready. The ball came fast, and I had to fight the urge to close my eyes, but at that moment, something else happened. Exhilaration.

Over the next few innings, I had more fun than I had ever had on the diamond. I was involved in every play, I had the best view on the field, and I felt like a bada$$ when I threw a runner out trying to steal second base. This was my softball calling.

Playing catcher played to *all* my strengths: no fear as the ball came at me at fifty miles per hour, not to mention the occasional foul tip; using my arm and quickness to throw runners out; and the eye-hand coordination needed to dig balls out of the dirt so they didn't reach the backstop, a strength I hadn't used as much on the field. As a huge plus, I got to hone my leadership skills as I called pitches. I wasn't the only one who had noticed that the combination of strengths was a huge asset to the team. Coach noticed too.

For the remainder of the season, I shared the catching duties with a teammate, but the next year, the position was all mine.

The lesson here is that playing to your strengths might take some trial, error, and perhaps a little luck, like being in the right place at the right time, as well as the willingness to get out of your comfort zone and take a risk. However, the reward might be just what you need but didn't know you were looking for. Sometimes we know we're not playing to our strengths, but in other cases, a chance encounter might be a game-changer.

5

Choose the Right Seat on the Bus

've worked with different companies over the years, and I've learned that everyone has a different definition of what a sales representative is, as well as a large variety of titles for those sales reps. As I like to say, "Titles are cheap and business cards are cheaper!"

There are as many types of sales positions as there are companies. Two or three times a month, someone I know will come to me and say, "Hey, I've got a friend looking for a sales job, would you mind talking to her to see if you can help?"

To which I always answer, "Sure, I've got thirty minutes for everyone. What kind of sales job is she looking for?"

The confused look on my friend's face tells me all I need to know. They think a sales job is a sales job, right? So the questioning (and the education) begins. Inside or territory rep? Hunting for net new business or taking on a book of business and growing and retaining it? Do they want to keep what they catch or give the fish over to someone else to clean and fry? I laugh as their eyes get big and they respond with, "Oh, I have no idea. Can you just give them a call?"

"I'd be happy to," I say.

The thing is when I do meet with this friend of a friend who is looking for a sales job, quite often they don't know how to answer those questions either. Which probably explains why so many people leave the sales profession, having decided it just "wasn't for them." They took a seat on the bus that wasn't the seat they could be happy in because they didn't know themselves, and they didn't know their options.

To further illustrate my point, I had a conversation with a woman just last week who was referred to me by a friend because she wanted a new sales job. I started down my usual list of questions and at the end, she said, "I don't mind hunting, but I want to keep the client after I land them."

"Perfect," I said. "That narrows the playing field considerably."

I love it when I can work with someone who knows what they want, knows what they're good at, and is willing to be honest with themselves and with me. I was so happy that she understood the type of sales position that would satisfy her. This will make her search much easier.

Just as confusing as understanding what type of sales jobs are out there is the variety of titles that companies use for those jobs. I've worked with account executives, account managers, regional directors, regional managers, sales associates, business development reps, inside sales reps, and more. And I can promise you that just because two people have the same job title, it doesn't mean they do the same job.

It's important as you look for a "sales job" that you don't make any assumptions based on title alone. You must read the job description and expectations; then you'll start to better understand what type of sales position it is.

Taking the wrong sales job will be frustrating, confidence-breaking, and could lead to failure. After you understand what all your options are, you then need to ask yourself, "Which sales position will best play to my strengths and skills?" The better you understand your strengths (which we'll spend more time discussing in a future chapter) and how you want to interact with prospects and customers, the easier this becomes.

Let me outline some differences between the two main sales position options, hunters and farmers:

Hunters (a.k.a. account executive, sales development reps, business development reps, regional directors)

- Love the chase
- Don't know a stranger
- Naturally curious (some may say nosy)
- No interest in continuing a relationship after the sale
- Money-motivated
- Risk-takers
- Love to be in control
- Enjoy the tension during the sales process

Farmers (a.k.a. account managers, customer/client success managers)

- Helpers and nurturers by nature
- Enjoy the process of getting to know someone over time
- Moderate risk tolerance
- Enjoy being a subject matter expert and always knowing the answer
- Like the consistency in their day-to-day work life
- Don't like the "sales tension"

Remember, as I shared in my Kristieisms, hunters aren't helpers and would prefer to just give birth and let someone else raise the baby. Farmers, on the other hand, wouldn't miss a milestone if their life depended on it.

When you know which role is best suited to your strengths and preferences, you can put yourself in the right position to become a true Rock Star. When you don't know, you're likely to find out the hard way.

Let me tell you about the time I made the mistake of hiring two sales reps for hunter roles, only to find out they weren't hunters at all. I was working for a SaaS company as the Director of Sales. The company was growing, and the owner and I decided it was time to add to the sales team, so I went in search of a few more hunters. I define a hunter as someone responsible for acquiring new companies as customers and then handing them off to someone else to grow and retain the account.

After interviewing several candidates, I made offers to these two women. Back then, and still today, it was very unusual to find women in the sales field who were natural hunters, and I was not only excited to be expanding the team but to be doing so with women no less! While onboarding, it was obvious they were smart, ambitious, and quick learners. They got off to a fast start and were doing a great job of prospecting and filling their pipeline with deals. I was very excited and happy with their performance. Of course, they needed some hand-holding to close a few deals, but I told myself that was to be expected.

Over the next few months, both women started to struggle. They weren't putting enough deals in their pipeline to reach their monthly quotas. I met with them more frequently, monitored more calls, and provided extra encouragement, yet they continued to underperform. I could feel their frustration, disappointment, and concern as they fell further behind their annual quotas. I, too, was concerned. Had I mis-hired them? Were they not up for the challenge?

Around the five-month mark, that voice in my head, the one I don't like to hear but have learned to listen to, told me the struggles the ladies were having were more than just newbie challenges. I sat down with the rep I felt I had the best relationship with and gave her what I affectionately call my "Mommy" speech. This is where I tell struggling reps they don't really seem happy, are clearly frustrated, and are spending more time at work than at home. I them they should wake up every morning happy to come to work. I suggest this isn't normally the case when reps miss their quotas.

"You don't seem to be enjoying the job as much anymore, am I right?" I asked.

She told me I was right. "I love it here. I love working for you, but I don't know what to do to be more successful, and I don't look forward to coming to work," she said.

"What part of the job *do* you enjoy?" I asked.

"I love talking to the prospects and learning about them and how they're training their employees," she said.

"What don't you like?"

"I don't like the prospecting, calling in to companies and trying to get past the gatekeeper," she shared.

Then it hit me! She was not a hunter; she was an account manager. I had mis-hired her! I put her in the wrong seat on the bus, as the book *Good to Great* by Jim Collins explains it. She most definitely belonged on the bus, but I set her up to fail by putting her in the wrong seat.

I moved both women to the Account Management team, where they flourished. In fact, I'm proud to say that seventeen years later, the woman I was closest to was promoted to CCO—Chief Customer Officer.

Let me break down my failure as the interviewer and how I could have better identified them as farmers earlier on. And how, if they had known themselves better and maybe read this book, they would have applied for roles that were better suited to their strengths and preferences.

One of the women had prior retail experience but not inside or phone sales experience. I now know, older and wiser, that those with retail experience sometimes rely on face-to-face and nonverbal cues to read their customers. Also, the type of retail sales she was doing provided for repeat business and allowed her to build a relationship with her customers over time. I could have asked more interview questions about her likes and dislikes about her job. Knowing what I know now, I'm sure she loved helping the same customers over and over again over the years—*account manager alert!*

Don't rely on an interviewer to determine if the role is right for you or not; you need to take responsibility for choosing a sales position you can be successful at.

I tell candidates during the interview process, "You should know before I do if this is something you will enjoy and can be successful at." Even though I take full accountability for mis-hiring those women, if either of them had had even one additional sales position under her belt before applying for the hunter role, she might have determined for herself that she wasn't going to be playing to her strengths.

There's one more type of sales role worth mentioning. These are the sales-support players who ensure that hunters, farmers, and the company are successful. These positions can be just as rewarding and challenging as a hunter or gatherer. Again, the better you know yourself, the easier it will be to decide if one of the following roles would be a good fit for you.

BDR/SDR (Business/Sales Development Rep)

This is a "starter" hunter sales job and is usually held by someone who is a year or two out of college. This position is responsible for setting up "discovery" appointments for the more senior hunters on the team. It is usually a base + bonus position and is a great way to find out if you like to hunt, as it is a pure hunter position. This position may be part of the sales organization or might be part of the marketing organization, as it is closely tied to lead generation. This is a great way to test drive the quota-carrying hunter position to see if it would be something you could be successful at.

Solutions Consultant/Sales Engineer

This position is part of the sales team and usually supports more than one hunter. In a more complex software sale, the hunter is not expected to demonstrate the software or understand all the technical complexities of the product. The SC's or SE's responsibility is to demonstrate the software being sold and act as the technical contact. This is a great position if you're technically inclined *and* an extrovert who brings a side of "helper" to the table. This is usually a base + bonus position and a great way to see if you might like hunting, as you'll be an integral part of the sales process.

Implementation/Onboarding Specialist

These individuals are responsible for onboarding new clients to the product or service. Think of them as the bridge between the hunter and the farmer. A new client might be assigned an implementation specialist for a few weeks as the product and technical post-sale specialist. Once the product is customized and up and running, the client is then moved on to their customer success or account manager, where they will live out the rest of their time as a client. This is a great way to test drive the farmer position to see if you'd like to manage, upsell, and renew customers on a daily basis.

If you're unsure if you are a hunter or farmer, take a minute and answer the questions below.

Hunter/Farmer Assessment
Questions (Yes/No)

1. Would my friends and family describe me as a risk-taker?

2. Do you love building a relationship over a long period of time?

3. Are you more likely to ask for forgiveness after making an "executive decision?"

4. Do you get satisfaction from caring for and nurturing others?

5. Do you thrive on competition?

6. Do you get satisfaction from helping others and being a trusted resource?

7. Do people sometimes call you nosy?

8. Are like to ask for advice from your manager before making a big decision?

9. If you miss your flight and need to stay at the airport hotel for the night are we likely to find you at the hotel bar chatting it up with other stranded travelers?

10. Do you love teaching someone something new?

11. Do you think a dial-by-name directory is just a game to be won?

12. Are you most comfortable with a base salary that will cover your living expenses?

13. Do you want full control over your income?

14. Are you more likely to ask for approval from your boss before getting back to a prospect about a discount?

Add up all the odd questions to which you said yes. Do the same with the even numbered questions.

If you answered yes to six or more odd numbered questions, **you're a true hunter**. You love the thrill of the hunt and closing deals and are always keeping score. Starting at zero every month doesn't bother you, and truth be told, it gets you out of bed each day. You are a risk taker and would be fine with 80 percent of your total compensation being uncapped variable/commission.

If you answered yes to four or five odd numbered questions, **you lean toward being a hunter** and would prefer that your compensation plan include a variable/commission component but are comfortable with your base salary being at least 50 percent of your total compensation. You like the challenge of closing deals but would prefer to keep what you catch to grow and expand the business.

If you answered yes to six or more even numbered questions, **you are a true farmer.** Your friends, family, and colleagues consider you a nurturer and look to you when they need a supportive ear and a shoulder to cry on. Your clients expect you to ask about their kids, vacations, and sick parents, and you're sad when your main client contact changes jobs and you are no longer in regular contact with them. You don't want the pressure of having to ask anyone for money.

If you answered yes to five or fewer even numbered questions, **you lean toward being a farmer** but wouldn't mind a job that gives you some commission or has a bonus plan based on renewing or upselling a client. You like helping others and enjoy getting to know your clients and being in regular contact with them.

Sales can be such a rewarding career. Each of the positions I've outlined in this chapter are important to the success of a company and can be extremely rewarding both professionally and financially. Think about the sales position you believe would be the most rewarding and where you could have the biggest impact. I encourage you to ask a few friends and family members if they agree, but ultimately, *you* are accountable for your success and happiness.

6

Choose Your Swim Lane

Now that you better understand what your options are for choosing the right seat on the bus, I'm hopeful that you're starting to get a feel for the direction your sales path will lead. I want each role you take and each company you join to get you one step closer to what will ultimately be what I call "your swim lane." This is the area of expertise you create and own, and it will ensure your success. Owning a swim lane is a more direct route to success. It sets you apart from coworkers and competitors alike. It will make the journey easier. It will increase your chances of success and the speed at which you get there.

World-renowned swimmer Michael Phelps, says, "Swimming is normal for me. I'm relaxed. I'm comfortable, and I know my surroundings. It's my home." That's how you should feel when you find your swim lane. Relaxed and completely comfortable in your surroundings. You should wake up every day saying, "I got this. I own this space, and no one can stop me from achieving my goals and the financial freedom that comes from being the best in my 'sport.'"

Your swim lane can include being an expert within an industry, with a type of product or service, in a region of the country, with the size of deals you choose to sell and/or the size of company you decide to sell to. Picking a swim lane not only makes you a subject matter expert, but it also makes your job easier. You'll get more referrals, you'll see trends and changes in the industry before others—thus, you will be able to react much more quickly than someone who isn't as attuned—you'll be given "A-Player" privilege by your boss and company, and so many more advantages.

The swim lane you develop should eventually provide you with the personal and financial freedom needed to create the life you want and deserve. Finding your swim lane isn't an event; it's a process, and it might take some time. You need to carefully evaluate each opportunity you take and each company you work for to make sure you get one step closer to finding your swim lane and the financial freedom that comes with it.

Let me share with you the evolution of how I found my swim lane. I went to college with no clue as to what I wanted to be when I grew up. What I did know was that I had writing skills (and enjoyed writing); I was competitive, a hard worker, and just sassy enough to be annoying at times to some people. So from the writing standpoint, it made sense for me to choose a major in journalism. Those classes were easy for me, and I enjoyed the curriculum, my professors, and my classmates. Now I needed to blend my writing skills with my competitiveness and brashness to see what jobs might be a fit for my skills and personality.

As it came time to graduate, two companies showed interest in hiring me. Interestingly, neither had anything to do with journalism. Both were department stores—Kmart (remember the blue light special?) and The Jones Store Co. (now Macy's). I received offers from both and chose to start my career with The Jones Store Co. out of Kansas City as a department manager in a store. I was excited and soon found that my strong work ethic, assertive personality, and competitiveness made me a perfect fit for retail.

After a couple of years working in the stores, I took a position as an assistant buyer with a different department store and transferred to St. Louis, Missouri. As an assistant buyer, I was responsible for a small segment of a larger department and had the opportunity to be mentored by an experienced buyer. Soon, I was promoted to a buyer position, and I got my own department to run and manage. This is where I honed my analytical and negotiation skills. In terms of sharpening your negotiation skills, there's nothing like dealing with Marty from Mudd, trying to get him to sell you 400 more pairs of a best-selling model of jean shorts, at a discount, in the middle of the summer.

After a couple of years as a buyer, I felt like a cog in the machine. There were so many management layers, and it took so much paperwork to get anything accomplished. I wanted to be more nimble and feel like I was making a difference. The rebel in me wanted to ask for forgiveness and not permission, but the company motto was "Get a partner." Not exactly the rebel cry I was longing for. There were also some decisions being made at the executive level that didn't align with my values, so I made the decision to leave corporate life behind and forge a new path.

When I set out to find my next opportunity, I had one goal in mind. I wasn't just looking for a new job, I wanted to find a company I could call home. I knew I had developed many business skills as a buyer that would be valuable to all kinds of companies, and I wanted to find the right place that would appreciate what I had to offer and align with my values. I ended up at a small privately-owned sales organization with about twenty employees. The owner, Dean Pichee, was looking for someone with more business experience and acumen than most of his staff had at that point, as well as someone who could help him grow the business by a few million dollars. It seemed like the kind of place where I could learn new skills and make a difference.

I jumped aboard without a title, not much of a job description, and no real idea what to expect. Over the next ten years, I helped Dean grow the business from $1M to over $8M, and we grew to over fifty employees. Over those ten years, I started to discover my swim lane. I fell in love with being at a smaller company, selling a software product, training sales reps, and then seeing them make more money than they thought they could. I also had the opportunity to build and lead the customer success team, where one of my biggest accomplishments was putting on our first client conference. I enjoyed being part of the executive team, making decisions that would help take the company to the next level. The education I received over those ten years was invaluable and just what I was looking for. I'm grateful that Dean took a chance on me and that I was bold enough to take the risk and make a hard left turn at the right time.

After ten years with Dean, I was ready for a new adventure. At this point in my career, I knew the following: I wanted to work for a privately-owned company; I loved software sales; I had strong leadership skills; sales needed to be part of my swim lane, and I needed to be around people smarter than me so I could grow and be engaged. I was getting closer to finding my swim lane.

I ended up as the director of Sales at a VC-backed technology company running a $28M department with over fifty employees. With fifty employees in two different states and five middle managers, this was a huge step up for me. I took this job because I wanted to work for the COO, Carl. I'll share more about Carl later, but for now, let's just say that as soon as I met him, I knew he'd make me a better leader and person—and I was right! This opportunity, although short-lived (I was only there for eighteen months as a result of the company being acquired by Web.com), helped me add one more missing piece to my swim lane puzzle. I learned that I thrived in a VC-backed environment.

There were a few reasons for this. When a venture capital company invests money in you, they expect a return. That adds pressure and a sense of urgency that I just haven't found in boot-strapped companies. VC-backed companies attract a certain type of person: smart, driven, and hardworking with a high-risk profile. The environment was electric each day. Decisions and the first move to execute those decisions seemed to happen in a split second. You have hours or days to execute, not weeks or months.

This opportunity added a little more clarity to what I wanted my swim lane to be: a sales leadership role at a SaaS software company, privately-owned and VC-backed, and that attracted top talent.

My next stop I'd actually call a detour. Despite knowing all the things I enjoyed and excelled at, I took a bit of a wrong turn with the next position. I exchanged my love of software to try my hand at CPG (consumer product goods). All the other components were there—sales leadership, privately owned/VC-backed with smart and motivated people. The CEO and COO had come from Breyers Ice Cream and had been hired by the VC firm (after turning around Breyers) to come in to grow this company and help them get ROI (return on investment). It didn't take long for me to realize the CPG just wasn't sexy enough for me. I missed software sales and wanted to be back in the B2B software world. So here's the lesson (you knew I had one, right?): When you realize you've made a mistake, #ownyourownshit and move on. I was in and out of that company in nine months. The mistake was necessary because it validated for me that software really was my passion and my swim lane. So we parted on good terms, and I got back into software sales.

The next position had everything I was looking for but wasn't VC-backed. This two-and-a-half-year stint helped me continue to hone my SaaS sales leadership skills with the new sales team while adding a position leading customer success back into my resume as well. The opportunity to run the entire revenue stream for a single organization was exciting and challenging, but I was missing that feeling you have when you're VC-backed. So . . . I #ownedmyownshit and made a change.

The next opportunity was the one everyone in the SaaS startup world longs to get. I was given the opportunity to build an SDR team from zero to twelve reps in less than three months at a heavily VC-backed company on track to be the first unicorn ($1B in valuation) in their category. This opportunity checked all the swim lane boxes! SaaS, startup, VC-backed, smartest executives ever, and based in Silicon Valley. Once, maybe twice, in your career as a sales leader will you ever get the opportunity to build a team from scratch. You own every hire and hiring mistake! What more could a girl ask for? Nothing! I had arrived. This was by far the most fun I'd had in my career—hiring twelve reps in under three months, training them, setting up all the processes, and motivating them daily to help the company reach triple-digit growth that first year. I didn't know the term "imposter syndrome" back then, but trust me when I tell you it was in full force in my head.

So when I decided to start a consulting business, everything I had done up to that point made the decision to focus my new business on helping early stage, VC-backed startups easy. That is my swim lane. It's what I love; it's what I understand, and it's where I can make the greatest impact for the founders who are fighting imposter syndrome, the board, and their competitors every day.

Knowing my swim lane and having a very specific target audience has made it easier to develop a go-to-market strategy. It's also made closing deals much easier, as most of my business comes from referrals, and it's made success happen more quickly, putting me in a position to expand my reach globally. When a founder is sharing their struggles with a VC or others in the startup community, they tell me they commonly get this advice: "That's what Kristie does. She can help you. Give her a call." I've now established myself as *the* startup expert.

So what's the first step you need to take to determine your swim lane? Start by asking yourself the following questions:

- What do I love about the positions I've had and the companies I've worked for?
- What industries do I gravitate toward?
- What am I better at than my coworkers and competitors?
- What products/services are easier for me to sell?
- What challenges are my coworkers facing when they come to me for advice?
- What do I tend to do better with shorter or longer more complex sales cycles?
- Do I prefer smaller companies with less structure or larger companies with many SOPs (standard operating procedures)?

Having a swim lane is all about focus. And answering these questions should give you an idea of where you need to focus, making a conscious decision to say yes to opportunities, people, and companies that can help you become a subject matter expert and no to things that won't help you own your swim lane.

Billionaire Warren Buffett, the chairman and CEO of Berkshire Hathaway, says, "The difference between successful people and really successful people is that really successful people say no to almost everything."

Having focus and saying no to things that won't help you establish your swim lane requires discipline and confidence in knowing that if you say yes to everything, you've really said yes to nothing. This means saying no to positions that will take your focus away from your specialty, no to working for companies that don't align with your values, and no to working for people who don't understand or agree with your vision.

Now that you know where to focus and where you're going to put your energy, let's dive deeper into what will set you apart from any other rep in the field.

7

Develop Your
Secret Weapon Strategy

I love a good competition. For thirteen years, I satisfied that love playing racquetball. I played in tournaments at the open level, and if I do say so myself, I was good! Then when I was twenty-eight, I became pregnant with my son. As my belly grew, it became harder and harder for me to get my racquet on that little blue ball when it was traveling just inches off the ground. At that time, I was playing twice a week with a girl I had grown up playing Junior Racquetball with, and she suggested we switch to tennis for the last few months of my pregnancy. I loved the idea and soon discovered I loved the game. By the time my son was born, I was wondering if tennis might be my next sport.

I've always excelled at eye-hand coordination sports—racquetball, softball, and volleyball—so tennis seemed like a good choice. Having played mostly singles in racquetball, I also liked that I could continue to play singles. So I started with group lessons to see how those would go.

After a few months focusing on the basics, I learned I had an unexpected secret weapon—my slice forehand. Thanks to my years of competitive racquetball, I have a natural and wicked forehand slice. It became obvious early on that what came naturally to me was also a struggle for others to learn: as an opponent, they had no idea how to handle a slice ball coming at them. My slice forehand is my secret weapon when it comes to tennis.

First, as we've already established, it's just as important for you to pick the right sales role as it was for me to pick the right sport. In this case, I knew my strengths and preferences; I have good eye-hand coordination, and I like the feel of swinging at a ball and connecting. So racquetball was a good fit. But tennis was also a great fit because the technique I developed for my racquetball game didn't just make me good at tennis, it made me uncommonly good. It gave me a secret weapon.

What's your sales secret weapon? The one skill or trait you count on to win the deal and outperform your competition, taking you into that Top 10 Percent status? It may be that, like my forehand slice, you have an edge that you've honed into an offensive advantage. Or like James, you may have developed a character trait to the *n*th degree to overcome or offset a personal challenge.

A secret weapon can be anything that makes you great with people, helps you connect the dots in a complex deal, makes you super diligent and dependable, or anything else that makes you just a *little* better at one or more areas essential to the sales role you've chosen. Whatever it is, define it, build a strategy around it, and deploy it.

Now that I had identified my tennis secret weapon, I just needed to develop a strength strategy around it to maximize its effectiveness. Even though it came naturally to me, I knew that if I further developed it, it could be the difference between winning and losing matches. I needed to develop the muscle memory that would make it second-nature, burn it into my reflexes, and take the thinking out of it. So I found a private coach and spent hours practicing and perfecting my slice so I could make my slice "move" more. Practicing your sales skills isn't any different.

I also learned to use that same slice stroke to disguise a drop shot. It was like a BOGO—buy a slice and get a drop shot for free! In the same way, you can learn to combine your secret weapon with another ability for an unbeatable combination.

After a couple of months of practice, I decided it was time to put my hard work to the test. I approached my group lesson instructor and told her I thought I was ready to test my skills in a more competitive way. I asked her what my options were, and she told me about USTA (United State Tennis Association) leagues. There are multiple teams made up of fifteen*ish* women, and each week they compete against other teams with three courts of doubles and two courts of singles. The team that wins the most courts wins the match. I loved the idea that my head-to-head match not only counted for my "rating," but I was also part of a team, not unlike being a part of a sales team. As it turns out, my instructor ran a USTA team and invited me to join. I loved the women on the team. They were supportive, like-minded, and enjoyed a cocktail or two after the match. It was perfect for me. A balance of cardio, competition, and cocktails!

It was in competition where I sensed my strength strategy was coming together. I saw opportunities on the court and different situations where putting my slice in play would dramatically increase my chances of winning the point, game, set, and, hopefully, the match! Having a sales strength strategy will increase your win rate as well, but you need to take it into "real life" situations to make it really work for you.

After playing tennis competitively for more than fifteen years now, the scouting report on my slice has gone viral, and even though most of the local singles players are well aware of my slice strategy, it still causes frustration from time to time and always throws off the women I play against when we travel out of town. I jokingly tell my opponents after the match when they bring up my slice that there's a monthly support group, and it involves cocktails!

Moving from a 2.5 rating when I started to a 4.0 singles player with a winning record today is my reward for all the hard work I put in for the first two years and the time I still put in today to maintain my rating. The keys to my success on the tennis court were:

- Picking the sport that most closely resembled racquetball, a sport I already loved and excelled at
- Transferring my strengths from racquetball to tennis, which then helped me identify my secret weapon
- Practicing and perfecting my slice forehand, which was my secret weapon
- Deciding to pressure test my secret weapon in a competitive situation
- Building a strategy around my secret weapon that I could count on when I'm struggling

Here's how that's going to apply to you as you set yourself up for success in a sales role:

1. Pick the right sport/job/role.

When I needed to find another way to stay in shape during my pregnancy, I could have picked any sport, but I reviewed my existing athletic strengths and determined that picking up another racket sport would be an easier transition than, say, deciding to learn how to play hockey. Sure, there were differences, a larger court, a longer racket, and a much different way of keeping score, but I knew I had some skills I had built while playing racquetball that would transition to tennis and that racquet sports let me take advantage of my natural gifts.

It is important that you spend time picking the correct type of sales role that might build off prior skills and jobs. Remember the woman I mis-hired for a hunter role? Well, if I had really thought about it, I would have realized her prior face-to-face retail experience, managing a cosmetics line, would probably make her a better account manager than hunter. Do the assessment offered in the previous chapter to make sure you're picking a "game" that plays to your strengths, lets you develop a secret weapon of your own, and gives you a real "zing" when you make that winning shot.

2. Pick the right team.

I've played with the same core group of women on the same tennis team for over ten years now. They're my teammates on match day, which is Sunday, but they're also the ones I turn to when I need someone to talk to or lean on. When my dad passed away unexpectedly, it was my teammates who showed up at my door with wine, food, flowers, and support. Everyone needs to be part of a team that is supportive and encouraging, and that you can count on to pick you up when you've lost a deal or are behind quota. The right company and team can be the difference in success or failure.

3. Identify your secret weapon.

You probably have several sales competencies you feel are strengths, but what *one* skill do you have that feels like your secret weapon? The one skill or trait that you can count on to be a game-changer for finding prospects and closing deals? Maybe you think you have an innate ability to pull information out of people that they wouldn't normally share or your negotiation skills are better than most, or maybe you feel your strength is holding prospects accountable. Take your list of skills and determine which one behavior or skill is your secret weapon.

4. Develop a strength strategy.

Now that you've chosen and practiced your secret weapon, it's time to create a strength strategy around it. You need to determine under what circumstances and situations you will use your secret weapon to have the greatest impact. Think back to the times when you successfully had a "win" as a result of using your secret weapon. There are going to be times when putting it in play will be more effective than others. When are those times? Who are the best people to use it on? And when in the sales cycle might it be a game-changer? Write these down and commit to putting your secret weapon in play when the right situations appear.

5. Find a coach.

This decision can truly be game-changing. When I approached my instructor to ask about more competitive options, I didn't know anything about leagues, tournaments, or teams. Deciding to join a team that my current instructor ran made good sense to me. She knew my strengths and weaknesses, and I was confident she would set me up for success, not failure.

6. Test, then pressure test.

The only way to guarantee that you can count on your secret weapon under pressure is to pressure test it. How do you do that? You put it in play when you're down 2–5 in the set. You need to be 100 percent certain you can count on it when you need it the most. When you have to add one more deal to the pipeline or close one more deal in the quarter to hit your bonus, that's when you double down on your secret weapon.

You're not going to really know for sure you can count on your secret weapon until the chips are down. Why? Because when everything is going well, you're relaxed and confident, and your performance is high. When you're behind quota or your pipeline is anemic, you're stressed, tense, scared, and worried. When you are feeling this way, everything takes more effort and is harder. You need to use a skill that you know won't let you down when you're feeling insecure, worried, or under pressure. That's when you pull out your secret sales weapon. Put it to the test. When it comes through like a champ, then you'll know that no matter how stressful the situation, you can count on it to pull you through!

Of course, success begets success, so once you've successfully executed your secret weapon, turn right around and use it again! You'll be surprised how quickly you'll be able to trust that success is guaranteed when you execute your secret weapon perfectly.

8

Gather Your Resources

At any point in our lives and careers, we actually have resources available to us we don't even notice. Those might be educational opportunities, like books, podcasts, or community training, and mentoring. Most often, the most valuable yet most overlooked resources for me were my relationships with people.

Just as I wouldn't be running my own company or writing this book if I hadn't built and nurtured my relationship with my former employer, Dean Pichee, you will find, especially in sales, it will be those relationships you genuinely invest in that give you the greatest return.

That's why, when I unexpectedly ended up managing a sales team, my first thought was, *Who do I know and who do I need to know?*

I joined a privately owned elearning SaaS company in 2000 as operations manager, fresh off the retail turnip truck. All I had ever done was retail; I'd never worked for a B2B (business-to-business) company before, and I definitely didn't know anything about operations. Apparently, I interview well, because here I was in an operations role. If the copier was jammed—that was me. Out of Post-its? Call Kristie. Questions about your health insurance? You guessed it: that was me as well.

About a year into my operations education, the owner approached me about running the sales team, which he was currently managing with a couple of team leads. Here we go again, jumping in with both feet. I knew nothing about running a sales team, but it sounded fun, so I said yes!

I knew I didn't know what I didn't know, so I called a recruiter friend of mine and told him my news. He was excited for me. "Don't get too excited," I said. "I'm really calling for a favor. I need to put together a group of other sales leaders of small, privately owned companies who also don't know everything so we can figure it out together."

Our group of six sales leaders convened for the first time a few weeks later. Over the next few years, we met monthly to tackle everything from compensation plans to how to handle maternity leave for a commissioned sales rep. This group became my support group, advisory council, good friends, and drinking buddies.

So when you're taking stock of the resources you have and need to make your sales role fun and successful, make sure you build your own sales support group. Sales is a very rewarding profession, but it can also be stressful and filled with rejection. You need to have a circle you can turn to when you don't know what you don't know and when you need a pick-me-up.

Another "human resource" you'll be looking for is someone who *does* know what you don't know. A good boss, mentor, or practice partner can be the difference between getting to 50 percent of your earning potential or 100 percent. There are a lot of factors that make someone a great resource, but the number one thing I look for in a boss or mentor is this: "Will they make me better at something I want to be better at?"

I've worked for several good bosses over the years, but no one has had as great an impact on me in a short period of time as Carl Boothby. Carl helped shape the sales leader I am today. I knew the first time I met him, over coffee, he would make me better. He had a confidence about him that I was drawn to. His background was impressive, and the opportunity was definitely the challenge I was looking for. Most importantly, I felt that not only would he make me better, I knew he wouldn't let me fail.

It didn't take long to confirm I'd made the right decision. Two weeks into my employment, after a particularly impressive revenue day the day before, Carl appeared in my doorway and said, "Great day yesterday!"

"Thanks, it really was," I said.

He then asked, "What caused the numbers to be so high?"

What? My team had just knocked it out of the park and you want to know why? I just stared at him. I had no idea. I was still basking in the glory of the day, like I did when I landed the perfect drop shot. It had never occurred to me to ask *why*. That's when I knew for sure I'd made the right decision; Carl was going to make me better!

By contrast, much earlier in my career, I passed on an opportunity to take a position as an Enterprise Channel sales rep for EMEA (Europe), a company on my dream company list. I had interviewed for two other positions at this company and hadn't made the cut. Then I got another opportunity. As you might imagine, I was super excited. Third time's a charm, right?

This company had been a vendor partner at the elearning company where I had spent ten years, so I knew a lot of people there. To be honest, I was even more excited about this position than the other two I had interviewed for because there was a former channel manager there who'd been assigned to the elearning company, and we'd become close friends—he was a mentor. I knew if I could just get the job, he'd help me get up to speed fast. I got past the first two interviews then was asked to meet with the VP of Channel at O'Hare Airport in Chicago. He and I both flew in that morning, and I met him for coffee inside the terminal. I was so excited; I knew all I had to do was to get past this one man and the job was mine!

He already knew me by reputation, but we'd never met. As he began to ask me questions, I got the sense he was just going through the motions. He wasn't digging too deep; it was more of a conversation than an interview. When it came time for me to ask some questions, I started with the easy ones about expectations, onboarding, the territory, etc. Then I asked the questions that were really important to me, like how he was going to make me a better sales rep and person. As he answered these questions, he indicated his plan to retire in the next couple of years. I got the distinct impression he was already coasting to the finish line.

The interview ended, and I knew the job was mine if I wanted it. The problem was, I wasn't sure I wanted to work for someone who wasn't going to invest in me and help me get to the next level. My next step had to be the right step, and I was no longer sure this was it.

I got a call later that night from my buddy at the company who said an offer was coming my way. I remember not being as excited as I should have been after having interviewed three times in the past two years in hopes of landing my dream job with my dream company. As promised, the offer came the next day, and I asked for forty-eight hours to consider it. I really didn't need forty-eight hours. I knew what my answer was going to be. I just needed forty-eight hours to get over the devastation of waiting that long and knowing I wasn't ever going to work for my dream company. By turning down the job, I knew I'd never get another chance to interview with them again.

I called the HR director two days later and politely turned down the job. It wasn't an hour later that my buddy called me in shock to find out why I had turned down a job with my dream company.

"He's not going to make me better," I said.

"What do you mean?" my buddy asked.

"He's just waiting to retire. He won't invest in me or my development. I need to look up to and respect the person I report to, and I don't think I'll be able to do that," I told him.

The funny thing is, I also lost a little bit of respect for my friend because I now understood he wasn't working for a Top 10 Percenter who pushed him to be better, and he seemed okay with that.

9

Get Real and Get Real Committed

That place where the rubber hits the road is also the place where the honest truth meets the day-to-day routine. You need to get real with yourself about three things: what you really want and how you define success, what you're really good at and love doing every day, and what you're really going to do and do well.

Let me give you an example of that last one. An important part of coaching reps is to "call monitor." This means I listen to call recordings to help reps improve their conversations with prospects. I like to monitor at least two to three calls a week per rep, more if a rep is in their first ninety days on the job.

A few years ago, Courtney was one of the new reps I was call-monitoring. I noticed that Courtney's call numbers were good, but she wasn't scheduling any appointments with prospects. I listened to the calls where the CRM indicated she had connected with a prospect. Imagine my surprise when, call after call, I heard the prospect answer the phone, then I heard a click. I was confused. Were the prospects hanging up on her before she'd even had a chance to introduce herself?

Upon more investigation, I discovered it was Courtney who was hanging up on the prospects when they answered, not the other way around. I was shocked, to say the least. Her onboarding had gone well. She was bright, articulate, and seemed eager to learn. *What's going on here?* I asked myself.

When I approached Courtney with my discovery and asked her why, she said that when the prospect picked up the phone, she just froze. Wow! I didn't see that coming. How awful a feeling to have someone answer and then just freeze up. I felt bad for her. She really wanted this job to work out and was excited about the opportunity, but in the end, it wasn't a good fit for her.

Phone fear is real, and if you have a fear or reluctance to speak with strangers, an inside sales job will be a challenge. There are plenty of other types of sales positions out there that don't require cold-calling prospects; maybe one of those would have been a better fit for Courtney.

It's certainly possible to overcome a weak spot and to work hard enough to get good at something that scares you right now. But whatever you do, don't kid yourself that just working harder *or* smarter is going to make up for being in a role that isn't a good fit.

But let's say you've picked the right sales role, you've joined the right company, you're working for a boss that supports and inspires you, you've identified your secret weapon, you've spent hours perfecting it, and you've created a written strategy of how and when you'll put it in play. You're committed. Success is guaranteed, right?

I'm not sure. Because I don't know how *you* define success. And that's the key to loving or hating a sales job. You have to know what success means to you. At the end of the day, you could be meeting all the metrics for job success, even be considered *the* Rock Star on your sales team, and be unsatisfied and unfulfilled if you aren't successful in your own eyes.

For me, the feeling of success in sales is the same visceral feeling I get in competition. When I'm on the court, especially in a tournament, there's no better feeling than watching my opponent's eyes get big and see their body try to react as they realize I've just hit a drop shot during a crucial time in the match, and they have no chance of getting to it. The confidence it gives me when I put my secret weapon in play, when I need a point the most, is immeasurable.

I want you to feel the same way about your success. The excitement and pride you'll have when that prospect you thought would never buy says yes, or when the client you've been nurturing renews or upgrades. It's the greatest feeling, and it makes the days when all you hear is *no* totally worth it.

As I said about using your secret weapon, success begets success. When you know what success means to you and how it feels, you'll continue building on that all the way to the top.

You might feel like we've already gone deeper than you expected, and maybe you're feeling more prepared than you ever have to build a career that will let you sell your way into any life you want. But we've only laid the foundation!

Being a Top 10 Percenter, or what I call a "Rock Star Rep," starts with you as a person. The next step is to build processes for winning at every aspect of this game we call sales. So if you're feeling pretty comfortable and confident with the personal foundation we've built in this section, let's move into Section Two, where we'll talk about the processes you have to build to sell your way *in*.

Before you continue to Section Two, I encourage you to download the companion workbook.
Click the QR code to download.

SECTION TWO

PRINCIPLES AND PRACTICES OF A ROCK STAR SALES PROCESS

Once you've found a role and company where you think you can be successful, it's time to get out there and fill that pipeline with prospects, right?

Not so fast. The true Rock Stars in sales, the reps who have learned to sell their way *into* their dream life, didn't get there without a personalized and dependable sales *process*.

I know you want to impress your boss, your peers, even yourself. And you want to get that money rolling in ASAP. But as tempting as it is to just get in there and start selling, you'll get further faster if you nail your process before you start calling on prospects.

This section is all about understanding what a Rock Star sales process looks like, why it matters, and how to build your process to leverage everything you learned about yourself in Section One so you can quickly rise to Rock Star status without working harder than the average Joe or Jill.

Every piece of your process can be broken down into three stages:

1. **Information.** Things you need to learn and knowledge you need to have access to. This will include everything from information about your product and market to insider information on your competition and power dynamics inside your company.

2. **Decisions.** Once you have collected the necessary information, there will be things you need to work out, figure out, and continually test and improve. For instance, methods for filling your pipeline, nurture strategies, and personal sales goals fall into this category as do strategies for skill development, career advancement, and network building.

3. **Actions.** When you have the information you need to make good decisions, the things you need to do, and the things you need to do dependably again and again become obvious. This will include systems, practices, routines, and habits, some of which will require discipline on your part and some of which can be automated.

Using quality information to make smart decisions about the actions you will put on autopilot either through discipline or automation not only gives you more dependable outcomes, but it also lets you identify what is or isn't working so you can refine, polish, and repeat your success strategies as you go along.

A process lets you take full advantage of the "work smarter, not harder" adage. When you have built your process around your secret weapon, swim lane, and motivation structure, it's personalized to you. Of course, the more you practice your process, the easier it gets. Just like muscle memory makes my backhand slice easier than it was when I started using it, your process may feel like work in the beginning, but the longer you repeat and refine it, the easier it becomes.

Finally, your process gives you an order of operations that allows for 80 percent or more of your decisions to be made in advance. That leaves more of your focus and energy free to be applied to personalizing and customizing, creatively dealing with the 20 percent of the sales cycle that you couldn't predict, and building meaningful relationships with decision-makers and influencers.

A Rock Star sales process is one you can rely on when times get tough or when you take a new sales position at a new company or seek a promotion at your existing company. Having a personalized process will help get you to your sales goal and give you the confidence you need to take on that new and exciting challenge.

When you've done the work in Section One to get to know yourself, designed your process around that self-knowledge, then honed it until it's as natural as making your morning coffee or brushing your teeth at bedtime, working your process will always feel like hanging out with a good friend. No matter how long you've been apart, you feel easy and comfortable the next time you're together.

Yes, creating a reliable and repeatable sales process will be a labor of love, but you'll reap the rewards over and over. So let's get started.

10

The Sales Information Framework— What You Need to Know

n Section One, you uncovered information about *yourself,* your strengths, and your preferences. That information will give you the ability to customize a sales process that builds and leverages your personal Rock Star traits and provides the opportunities for you to be rewarded in ways that are most satisfying to you. It is going to help you make decisions and create action plans that give you the greatest advantage of selling your way to success on your own terms.

In this section, you're going to learn the types of information you need to gather to customize a sales process for any role, company, or product to give you the greatest advantage in meeting the sales goals you set for yourself to underwrite that success. With that information, you can make decisions and set up systems and automations for many of the actions required, leaving you free to get creative about taking action to meet the occasional curveballs that are inevitable in any sales success story.

The information you will need to gather to create that dependable success formula we call a "process" follows a universal framework. This framework is the same, no matter what sales role you are in or what product or service you're selling.

The central element in your framework is the **prospect** or **customer profile.** The information you gather about the company's ideal customer gives context to everything else. Until you have deep intel on your ideal customer profile (ICP), any other information you gather won't really be meaningful or useful.

Once you know how to identify your ideal customer or client and you understand their pains, fears, and vision, there are four quadrants of information you'll need to build: Product (and/or Service); Industry; Tools; and Strategies.

Comprehensive information in each of the four quadrants filtered through the lens of the ideal customer profile completes the foundation on which you will create and formulate your own personal sales process. This framework will be your key to quickly and systematically nail your sales process, no matter where your sales career takes you.

THE SALES INFORMATION FRAMEWORK

PRODUCT / SERVICE
> founder's story
> product evolution
> demonstrations
> customer benefits
> problems the
product solves

INDUSTRY
industry associations <
trends / challenges <
industry evolution <
ecosystem <
influencers <
competition <

IDEAL CLIENT PROFILE (ICP)
demographics
psychographics
firmographics
buyer personas

STRATEGY
> prospecting
> discovery
> sales cycle
> negotiation
> nurturing
> reputation
> skill building

TOOLS
CRM <
automation <
analytics <
artifical intelligence <
meeting schedulers <
data clean up <
electronic signature <

When onboarding a new sales rep, I make sure the client I'm working with knows that, in addition to a description of the company's ICP, these are the four primary areas they will need to provide training on. Of course, you may not land at a company that has a "Kristie," so you may not have this information at your disposal from Day One. If that's the case, this book was written for you!

My clients are prepared to train their new reps in this sales framework. But I still teach new reps to dig in and do their own information gathering before they make decisions about their process. This is really for two reasons. One, if they bring curiosity and a fresh perspective to the information they uncover, everyone is likely to learn something that was previously overlooked. And two, I want the rep to connect the information they learn to what they know about themselves before they make decisions about their personal sales process.

But whether you get a head start during your training or not, whether you are new to the role or looking to propel yourself to Rock Star status in a job you've held for some time, that information is there, and I'm going to teach you how to find it. Everything from the common characteristics of the ideal customer to the features, functionality, and benefits of the product or service you will be selling, how that product fits into the industry's ecosystem, the company's sales strategy or GTM (go-to-market) plan, and what tools you have available to you so you can be more effective and efficient while prospecting, moving prospects through the sales cycle, and managing them after the fact can be discovered and documented if you know how to go about it.

Let's take a look at each of these quadrants in more depth.

11

Know Your Ideal Customer Profile

"If you don't choose your clients, they will choose you!"

n sales, you need to deeply "get" two people; yourself and your ideal customer profile (ICP).

One of the most important things you'll do in building your process is to make sure that you understand who you *should* be selling to rather than who you *could* be selling to. And not just understanding who they are, but understanding them, their goals, their pains, their fears, their preferences, where they hang out, who they listen to--everything.

The goal of truly understanding your ICP is so you can spot them coming a mile away on a sunny day and bring them in for a soft landing. Conversely, if they aren't your ICP, you can turn and run away as quickly as possible.

Why would you run from a potential sale? Selling to the wrong prospect is costly. It will cost you and your company time and money, and it won't make your prospect a happy camper either. Selling to non-ICP prospects will result in extra time for support and higher churn. Not to mention that whether they buy from you or not, if they weren't a match for what you're selling, there is little to no chance they will be a promoter of your business.

On the other hand, when you have a clear understanding of your ICP, you can target higher value prospects, have better conversations, put more deals into the pipeline, and benefit from a higher close rate. When you can narrow your efforts to the *best* prospects and close them as quickly as possible, everyone is happier, wealthier, and better served. You've made the best use of your time and energy, your company has a client who will benefit highly from the purchase they just made, and the client will not only enjoy the benefits of the product or service, but they'll appreciate the ease with which they were able to make the purchase. Win, win, win.

Knowing your ICP goes further than simply identifying a prospect as a fit. The information you gather in this step is also essential to the decision phase when you interact with prospects. You'll use it to determine which prospects should be added to your pipeline, which need to be nurtured, and which don't fit your ideal customer profile after all and can be thrown back into the water.

A Rock Star sales rep learns to quickly discover not only the common traits and stats of the company's best customers, they also know to find out what makes these people tick, how to meet them "where they live," how to gain a reputation as their trusted resource, and how to develop lasting relationships with them, leading to greater customer satisfaction and loyalty, as well as higher probability of repeat business and referrals.

Generally, the more similar the prospect is to your company's existing customers (similar employee count, revenue, and industry, for example) the more likely they will be to purchase, the easier your job will be, and the more success you will have.

That means the first place you'll go to understand your ICP is your existing customer base. Even if your company has a documented profile of who they think their best prospect is, do your own homework. They might have completed that documentation when the product was in an earlier stage of development, the market might have changed since they last examined their ICP, or you might spot something they missed or that is only relevant to you because you can leverage your secret weapon or swim lane to greater success by narrowing the ICP description.

You should be able to identify common characteristics of companies and people within those companies (I'll refer to them as contacts going forward) who have purchased from the company in the past. This will help you determine who is most likely to purchase your product or service in the future.

We are looking for commonalities around things like industry, who the prospect's customers are, the number of employees they have, what region of the country they operate in, or the amount of revenue they generate each year.

All of these data points will give you clues to the types of companies you'll want to prospect. So how do we go about determining the ICP for your product or service, and more importantly the ICP with which you will have the highest sales success rate? We're going to look at several characteristics: demographics, firmographics, psychographics, and buyer personas.

How important each of these are to your business will be determined by whether you're selling business-to-consumer (B2C) or business-to-business (B2B). This book is written primarily from the perspective of B2B sales, as it is the more complex structure and one that is my personal swim lane. If you're selling B2C, some of these categories and tips won't be meaningful, but the basic principles still apply to you.

Let's start by defining each of these terms:

Demographics

Demographic information is all about the people who might purchase from you.

- Age
- Gender
- Occupation
- Ethnicity

- Geolocation
- Education level
- Religion

This will be important to you if you're selling directly to consumers. But it's also important information to gather about the company roles and decision-makers who will be your make-or-break contacts in the companies you're selling to.

Psychographics

Psychographic information is also about your buyers, but you aren't looking for facts like demographics. This is about what's important to people.
- Personality characteristics
- Lifestyle
- Social class
- Attitudes
- Principles & beliefs
- Activities & interests

This information helps you determine what social groups your ICP is likely to be part of, what relationship and trust builders are likely to be meaningful, and what they are most likely to value about your company and product as well as about you as their primary contact.

Firmographics

Firmographics information is about the company itself. This information will be most important if you're selling B2B, but if you're selling B2C and your ICP is likely to be in a business or professional role, some of this information will be relevant to your process.
- Industry

- Number of years in business
- Number of employees
- Annual revenue
- Location of headquarters and/or other offices and properties
- Type of organization (public, privately held, benefit corporation, etc.)
- Fortune rating (if applicable)

Buyer Personas

Buyer personas are fictional, generalized representations of your ideal customers. Personas help us internalize the ideal customer we're trying to attract and allow us to relate to our customers as real humans. We give them cute names like AP Alice, VP of Sales Sally, or Soccer Mom Sue.

This is one area where you can leverage *your* personal sales profile by deciding which buyer personas you most closely align with and focusing on reaching out to those individuals. This might even become your swim lane. Look for commonalities between your interests, experiences, and values and those of the buyers and decision-makers within certain industries or in different roles within the company.

I recently trained a large group of new SDRs who was tasked with qualifying contacts within the cyber security industry. There were really two types of buyers for security: those who worked in risk and security and those who were in the IT networking and security area. I shared with the SDRs that they would probably connect better with one group or the other, and as such, they should reach out to both initially and see whom they had the best conversation with, and then focus on those personas.

You want to understand the following about your buyer personas:

- What a day in the life of that person might look like
- How they are reviewed and held accountable
- What their career path looks like
- What keeps them up at night
- What their job responsibilities are

You can go even deeper into building your persona if you are selling B2B and know who your decision-makers and influencers will be by asking questions about:

- Role
- Department (revenue or cost department)
- Gender
- Age
- Challenges
- How do they advance/get evaluated
- Who they report to
- What outcomes they own

When gathering information about your ICP, your first source of information within your organization should be the account management team, customer success managers, or your sales manager. Enlist their help breaking your current customers into two lists: the ten best clients and the ten clients they wish they had never sold to. You can use criteria, such as how much the client has spent with the company, how many referrals they've sent your way, how much time/effort the company has had to invest to keep them happy, even how much of a joy (or pain in the neck) they've been to work with.

Learn all you can about what the clients on each list have in common using the demographic, psychographic, firmographic, and buyer persona criteria above.

The information you gather about your ideal customer and your personal ideal buyer persona are truly central to helping you successfully complete your framework, so go deep and be diligent, and you'll make your job easier and you'll be much more successful!

Homework for Knowing Your Ideal Client Profile:

- Schedule time with your Account Management, Customer Success, or even your Customer Service team to better understand, from their perspective, which customers they love to work with and are getting value and which customers aren't getting value and will never recommend your product to others.
- Document the information you gather, noting trends and commonalities among the highest value customers.
- Write out your personal ICP—the companies you think you will have the most success selling into.
- Write out which personas you think you can connect and relate to on a personal level to have the best chance of closing the deal.

12

Know Your Product or Service

"A half-baked product is worse than one that's still raw."

often tell clients that I can fix a broken sales process, under-trained sales reps, or a set of inefficient and under-customized sales tools. But I cannot fix a broken product. That's how important it is that your product or service is something that can be competitive in the market and that you can be successful selling.

So, before you take that next sales opportunity, make sure you've done your homework on the product or service your sales success will depend on. I work with startups, and I know when a product is still "raw," there's still every chance of building a hugely successful sales team because you're being upfront about the product's development stage. But if the product is "half-baked," and you're expected to sell it as deliciously done, you're doomed.

Hopefully, the product or service you've chosen to sell isn't broken *or* half-baked but has a strong value proposition, is something you can be passionate about, and is something you think you will be successful selling. If not, you might consider moving on to your next opportunity. If so, it's important you understand why the product was built, the benefits customers will see, and what other options might now exist for them to choose from.

When I onboard new sales reps, one of the first sessions I schedule for them is to learn something I call "The Founder's Story." I want them to understand why the founder of the company thought the product or service they built would be beneficial to others and help them solve a problem. This is because I want them to understand the evolution of how the product or service came to be and how it went from an idea to a reality.

My favorite founder stories usually sound something like this: "I was working for 'The Man,' and I kept bumping up against an inefficient way to do X, or I needed a better way to do Y. So I went out into the world to see who had come up with a way to solve the problem I was having, and I either couldn't find anything, or what I found solved some of my problems but not all of them. So I thought to myself, *If I'm having this issue, other people who do what I do or work in my industry must also be struggling.* I then decided to solve it myself and sell the solution to others like me and that's how Jones, Inc. got started."

Once you understand why your original founder chose to build the thing you'll be selling, you need to understand how the product or service has evolved since that initial offering. Most products will change, improve, and mature over time. These evolutions usually revolve around increasing the number of features or services, better usability, prettier packaging or customer interfaces, or more use cases or integrations. Make sure you understand where your product has been and where it is today.

As a result of a product's evolution, the problems the product or service solves have probably changed as well. You need to understand what issues the product solves for prospects and customers today. It's likely there are now several problems that can be solved by your product or service. Make sure you understand all the issues your product addresses before diving deeper into the product itself.

After you understand the problems the product solves, you need to understand all the features of the product or service and how those features directly tie to benefits the customer will receive. Unfortunately, most demos and presentations I audit focus on the features but fail to articulate how the benefits of that feature tie directly back to the issues the prospect is struggling with.

Prospects and customers won't care about your bells and whistles if they don't understand how ringing that bell or blowing that whistle will make their life easier. So make sure you can explain what a specific feature's corresponding benefit is.

No product is perfect, and the one you're selling won't be either. You need to know its shortcomings and flaws so you will be prepared to handle any objections you may receive because the product doesn't do everything a prospect might want it to do.

Once you are clear on the features and benefits of your product or service, you need to understand all the use cases a person might have for using the product. A *use case* is just a specific situation where your product could be used. The more deeply you understand your product's functionality and use cases, the more creative you can be when you have a prospect who doesn't at first glance, doesn't appear to fit your ICP.

For example, I consulted for a company that provides a workspace management platform. This product provides companies a way for employees to reserve a workspace or conference room for the time and day they need. As a result of the pandemic, this product gained interest rapidly. There were several use cases for this product:

- Reduce the capacity allowed in the office to ensure the health and safety of employees
- Track visitors who enter the building/office for contact tracing purposes
- Ensure employees who need to collaborate will have space to do so
- Allow the company to reduce the amount of real estate needed, thus reducing that expense

Recently, a sales rep at this company got a new and unusual use case. An organization contacted this rep and wanted to know if they could track and manage seventeen boats, which they kept at a nearby marina.

This wasn't what the product was originally built for, and if the rep had been considering only the ICP and not the proven use cases, they might not have pursued the lead. But this rep knew the product was designed to handle this situation, even though it had not been used for this application. They told the prospect that although the software was usually used for desk or occupancy management, boat management was entirely possible too!

You may not only need to know how to *explain* the features, functions, and benefits of your product, but you may also be required to demonstrate them. Regardless if you'll be required to demo your product by yourself or have a technical coworker (sales engineer or solution consultant) who will provide this service for you, you need to be familiar with how to do a demonstration of the basic features and functionality in the event that help is not available—or while on a call that is not intended to be a demo, but one on which a product question comes up.

Whether or not giving demos is part of your usual responsibilities, I recommend you are always prepared to give a demo if that's what is needed to move the prospect along. I also recommend that you ask someone who is involved in building the product, as well as someone in each department that uses, designs, or markets the product, to demonstrate it for you so you have perspectives and insights from someone who's been selling it.

As you can see, understanding your product or service, how it came to be, the problems it solves, what the use cases are, and how to demonstrate its functionality and value to prospects needs to be part of your training when you take a new job or take on selling a new product.

Homework for Knowing Your Product or Service:

- Be able to tell your founder's story to prospects and customers.
- Understand the product's or service's evolution.
- Understand the problems your prospects have that your product or service solves.
- Understand the value your offering brings a company.
- Be able to tie the benefits back to specific features.
- Keep a running list of use cases.
- Understand the demo process; make your plan to learn to demo, if necessary.

13

Know Your Industry

"No one gets on board with what you're selling until they believe you know why they're buying."

Now that you understand your product, you need to dedicate time to understanding your industry and the companies that make up your industry. Knowing that their Rock Star rep. understands what they're selling is just one tiny piece of the prospect's perspective, beliefs, and opinions on the purchase they're making. Being an expert about your industry is one way to gain insight into your IPC's point of view and gain the advantage in networking, prospecting, and closing the sale.

A book I recommend is *The Challenger Sale*. This book really speaks to the concept of a sales rep's responsibility to educate their prospects. This book makes it clear why it's *your* responsibility to educate your prospects on industry trends, introduce them to others in the industry who would be of value to them, and help them be a leader in their space. You can't do this if you aren't continually and consistently studying and immersing yourself in your industry.

Challengers aren't so much world-class investigators as they are world-class teachers. They win not by understanding their customers' world as well as the customers know it themselves, but by actually knowing their customers' world better than their customers know it themselves, teaching them what they don't know but should.
—From The Challenger Sale

Experienced buyers will expect that you understand the industry, including trends, challenges, and influencers. They'll also expect you to have built a network of industry insiders and experts. You'll also need to gain an understanding of your company's place in the industry's ecosystem and how your product or service fits into that ecosystem. Finally, having an in-depth knowledge of your industry will help you stand out as more informed, more credible, and more helpful than the average sales rep. That's not just my opinion, by the way. Training Industry, Inc. and Value-Selling Associates conducted a study to examine how business-to-business (B2B) sales interactions are perceived by buyer companies and found that 75 percent of buyers say sales reps don't demonstrate knowledge of their industry structure, and only 37 percent of buyers say sales reps provide unique industry insights.

We'll go deeper into creating a personalized action plan for staying in the know about your industry but remember that it won't be enough to just do some industry research as you're ramping up at a new company. The most successful reps understand they need to become part of the industry's community as well. It's that level of commitment and involvement that will set you apart from 67 percent of all other sales reps.

Staying abreast of industry trends will allow you to build trust and credibility with your prospects as you ask smart and strategic questions, such as, "Mr. Prospect, I've been following Ms. Expert, and she recently posted that she's noticing a shift in X. How is your company preparing to address this shift?" I tell sales reps the harder the question they ask, the more comfortable they must be with silence. It's entirely possible that you just informed your prospect of a trend they weren't aware of and haven't given any thought to. But they will now see you as a resource and expert whom they can rely on going forward to be a trusted advisor and not just a sales rep.

As Mark Twain is famous for saying, "There are no new ideas," but industry experts are keenly aware of shifts happening in the industry and will always have an opinion about what those shifts or trends will mean for the future of the industry in the short and long terms.

You can follow your industry's experts and influencers on LinkedIn and X, by listening to their podcasts, or reading what they've published as a contributing writer for an industry publication. There are also groups you should probably follow on LinkedIn, hashtags to follow on X, and industry podcasts to subscribe to. Having a channel push information to you and following the people "in the know" is much easier than constantly going out to find it.

Subscribing to industry magazines, newsletters, and blog posts is also a great way for you to be one of those people in the know. These are written by those who are keeping an eye on what's happening in your industry. They will not only help you stay on top of trends, as we've discussed, but they will also help you stay aware of industry events, such as educational training, conferences, and networking events.

One of the best ways for you to immerse yourself into your industry's community is to join your local or national industry association. These are *your* people, and you can regularly meet and discuss what you're seeing happening in your industry. As an example, I'm not only a part of the SaaS (software as a service) community, but I'm also a member of the AAISP (American Association of Inside Sales Professionals). It's not only important for me to stay on top of the SaaS industry, to be a resource for the startup founders I work with, but I also need to stay on top of new sales strategies and trends.

There are plenty of ways for you to not only become an industry expert and an expert on your craft, but also an expert on your competitors. Find what works best for you, whether that's listening to a weekly podcast or attending an association event quarterly. You want your prospects and customers to see you as a trusted resource for your product, your industry, and current trends.

Although I've been referring to competitors as other companies with a competing product, I actually define a competitor as anyone or anything that a prospect might spend money on to solve their issue. Using this definition, a competitor might not be as obvious as you think. Competitors tend to fall into two categories: direct and indirect.

Direct competitors are other companies that provide a similar product to yours. There are likely several players in your space that you need to familiarize yourself with. Much like you would go to Glassdoor to find out about a company before you apply for a job with them, if your prospects are using a source to gain information about your company and your product, you should be using the same source to learn what's being said about your product and your competitor's product.

Good places to get this information are other sales reps who have been selling for a while; everyone's friend, Google; and more targeted websites like G2, Angi, and Gartner that are aimed at your buyer. All these sites will list the vendors in your space and provide comparisons and ratings based on their own research and customer feedback.

Indirect competitors are less obvious but just as important to research and understand. An indirect competitor can be a company that has a product with a feature that might solve some, but not all, of the issues a prospect might have. Another indirect competitor could be the company's internal development team. Often an internal development team will lobby to build the product themselves so it's completely customized to their specific situation. There are downsides to having a proprietary system built internally. It usually takes a long time to build; it will need to be maintained by the team that built it, and it probably won't be enhanced as frequently as an "off-the-shelf" option. We call this the "build vs. buy dilemma."

For most of my clients, I recommend something referred to as a "battlecard." A sales battlecard is an internal document or spreadsheet, typically a one-page cheat sheet of high-value talking points created specifically to help your sales team address the differentiators of the competitors in your space. In fact, a 2022 State of Competitive Intelligence report found that 71 percent of businesses that use battlecards say they've increased their win rates as a result. If your company doesn't have one, I would suggest you and a few of your fellow sales create one—it will benefit everyone. And if your company does have one, I suggest you take the time to study it, update it, and meet with your fellow reps to see how you can improve upon it.

Homework for Knowing Your Industry:

- Join an industry group.
- Follow your industry's influencers.
- Join your industry's association.
- Understand where your product fits into your industry's ecosystem.
- Attend industry events, conferences, and tradeshows at least quarterly.
- Know your competitors. Put a battlecard together.

14

Know Your Strategy

"A good product won't survive a broken process."

J ust like it will be nearly impossible for you to successfully sell a half-baked or broken product, your company's sales strategy can be the difference between your success and failure as a sales rep. If your company's GTM (go-to-market) or sales strategy is flawed, then it won't matter how gifted a salesperson you are; you will struggle.

Sales strategies fall into seven general categories:

1. Prospecting: how leads are acquired
2. Discovery: how information is gathered and leads are qualified
3. Sales cycle: the process that you and your prospect go through to determine if they should become a customer
4. Negotiation: how items you and your prospect aren't in agreement on are worked out
5. Nurturing: how you provide value and stay top of mind with prospects before and after they buy
6. Reputation: how you build a reputation in your industry and community to increase influence, connections, referrals, and trust

7. Skill-building: how you improve your professional development through ongoing training, education, and mentoring

In the decision phase of setting up your process, you'll combine the information you gather about the company sales strategy with what you learned about yourself in Section One to create your personalized Rock Star sales process. But first, let's start with what you need to learn to move to that next step.

Homework for Determining Your Overall Sales Strategy:

- Decide on a sales methodology to use as your framework.
- Determine what sales training your company is providing and the training you will need to seek for yourself.

---

1. Prospecting Strategies

I hope your sales leader has put a successful and repeatable prospecting strategy in place for you and the team, but take it from me, there are way too many companies that seem to think the prospecting fairy is going to show up and wave her magic wand, and prospects will just appear out of thin air. The good news is this: even if your company doesn't have a formalized strategy, good information gathering will allow you to figure out what they're doing now so you can adopt what works and personalize what doesn't.

You've already done the work to figure out what your ICP looks like; now you need to figure out how you're going to connect with them. Will you be getting inbound leads from marketing? Will you have sales development reps (SDRs) pre-qualify and book appointments for you? Will you need to do your own outbound prospecting? Will you attend events to connect with them? Or is there another strategy your company employs to find your future customers?

Ask your manager and other reps which lead sources have been most likely to close in the past. By *lead source,* I mean, how did the lead come into the pipeline—did the prospect find you through your website or at a conference, or did you find them by outbound prospecting or having a former client refer them to you? Each lead source will most likely close at a different rate, so in the interest of working smarter, you should start by understanding which sources produce leads most likely to become customers and go after those.

Some of this is common sense. If a long-standing customer refers a prospect to you, it's more likely they will close—and close more quickly—because they received an endorsement from someone they trust. On the other hand, cold outbound prospecting might close at a lower rate and might also take longer to close.

Once you've figured out where most customers came from, you need to cross-reference this information with what you think the most effective way would be for *you* to find prospects, based on your past successes and secret weapons. Are you a persuasive and compelling writer, making email your strength? Can you charm the gatekeeper to put you through to the person you're trying to reach? Do you tend to perform better face-to-face at trade shows? Prospecting is hard, so this is definitely an area you want to play to your strengths.

Homework for Prospecting Strategy:

- Document all existing prospecting methods.
- Determine the prospecting methods that will best play to your secret weapons and sales superpowers.

2. Discovery Strategies

I'm finding more and more companies aren't teaching sales soft skills to their sales reps. Sometimes it's because the sales leader doesn't know *how* to train on sales soft skills. In other cases, it's because they don't truly understand the importance strong of sales soft skills in giving their reps a greater chance of success. Sales leaders have become heavily dependent on sales data, analytics, and automation tools to help them manage their sales teams. As these tools have gained popularity, the good old-fashioned sales skills training has gone by the wayside.

Regardless of *why* your company may fail to provide the soft skill training you need, mastering soft skills will be part of building your tool kit. So start by learning what type of professional development your company is or isn't offering around true sales soft skills. This isn't product training, CRM training, or how to fill out a contract. This is how to effectively and persuasively communicate with a prospect or customer in a way that will build trust so you can determine if there is a true fit between their needs and your product or service. If you're company doesn't provide sales training, then you'll need to take that responsibility on to make sure you are prepared to be as successful as you can be. Whether you're getting training support from your employer or you're on your own, I suggest you start with learning how to do proper discovery.

"Discovery isn't an event; it's a process."

Most companies will refer to discovery as a call or step in the sales process. I disagree. Discovery should happen during *every step* of the process. You'll not only be able to determine at any stage that a prospect isn't a fit for what you sell, but you'll also be building trust with the prospect and gathering vital information about their needs, values, and concerns.

Discovery, first and foremost, is about the prospect or customer. It has nothing to do with you or your product or service. Discovery happens when you take the time to ask questions that will help you determine if the prospect has a pain that your product or service can solve, that they want to solve, and that they're willing to spend money to solve.

I break discovery questions into two buckets: tactical and strategic.

Tactical

I refer to these as "housekeeping" questions. These are questions that have concrete and objective answers. Questions such as:

- How many employees do they have?
- How many locations?
- How much revenue are they bringing in?
- Who are their customers?

Strategic

These questions are harder to answer and can be more subjective, based on who in the company you're speaking with. These questions normally relate to why they have the problem they are trying to solve, what have they done to try and solve it, and why they believe what they've tried hasn't worked. Questions such as:

- What have you done to try to address the problem?
- What do you think kept that solution from working?
- What is the financial impact the issue is having on the business?
- What would need to happen for you to try solving the problem again in a different way?

There are a few places you can go to help you determine the type of discovery questions you should be asking if discovery training isn't being provided by your sales leader.

- Your sales leader: just because they aren't training on discovery doesn't mean they don't know the questions you should be asking
- The top sales reps: these coworkers are hitting or beating quota, so we have to assume they understand how to determine pain and if their product or service alleviates that pain.

- Customer success/account managers: these teams work with the customers after the sale and should have a handle on what problems the company was trying to solve and why they needed to solve them

An online class on discovery should provide you with a good overview of the types of questions you should be asking; then you'll just need to customize those questions for any situation that is out of the ordinary.

I teach a technique I call "Question on a Question" to make the discovery process sound more conversational. Start by asking the prospect a general open-ended question, such as, "Tell me about your current situation with X." No matter what the answer to your question is, you then want to ask a more specific question around the answer they gave. You continue doing this until you've uncovered a pain point or have determined they don't have a pain you can solve, or until you realize they aren't interested in solving the problem. Asking questions to seek to better understand will help you establish trust and find fit more quickly.

Homework for Discovery Strategy:

- Create a list of discovery questions you'll need to ask throughout the sales process to help you determine "fit."

3. Sales Cycle Strategies

Managing your sales cycle is both an art and a science, as are most things related to sales. You need to understand how many different stages there are in the sales cycle, how long each stage should take, and what criteria are used to move the prospect to the next stage. But the very first question you should ask is whether or not the organization uses a specific sales methodology. A sales methodology is a framework that provides actionable steps during every stage of the sales process. It takes the sales process and creates actions you should take to ensure the best results. Having a formal sales methodology allows the team to have a common language they use as well as consistency with how prospects and customers are moved through the process.

Here are some popular and common methodologies your company might be using:

- SPIN Selling
- The Challenger Sale
- The Sandler System
- MEDDPICC
- Solution Selling
- GAP Selling

Which methodology your company is using to guide the sales process is less important than knowing they are using *something*. If your company has adopted a methodology, you just need to understand how training on this methodology takes place and what resources are available to help you master the methodology.

Unfortunately, it's possible the organization you're working for isn't using a formal methodology to assure consistency and set you up for success, so it will be up to you to find a methodology that fits your selling style and then seek your own training. I advise you to look at methodologies provide a book, online class, or seminar you can attend so you'll learn from a qualified instructor and have some support as you're adopting the methodology and integrating it into your personal sales process to make sure you can leverage your sales superpowers.

A formal methodology will provide you with a framework, but you'll still need to customize the framework to your specific sales situation. For example, the framework might outline for you the different stages in the sales cycle and what should be accomplished in each stage, but it won't tell you how long each stage will last since that will be specific to what you're selling. So, even if you select a methodology you like and you believe will provide a strong framework for your sales process, expect to customize it to your particular situation.

You also need to understand that the sales cycle and the buyer's journey don't always coincide. The buyer's journey is the process the buyer goes through to determine what and if they will make a purchasing decision to solve an issue they are having.

The buyer's journey looks like this:

- Problem identification
- Solution exploration
- Requirements determined
- Solution selection

It's commonly understood that buyers don't really want to engage a salesperson until they are about 60 percent to 75 percent of the way through their buying process. Thanks to the internet, buyers are more informed than ever before and often don't need salespeople to discuss benefits, features, differentiators, or even pricing.

You should make sure you understand the buyer's journey for your specific product or service to ensure you can be most effective and helpful when the time is right for you and the prospect to begin working together.

Homework for Sales Cycle Strategy:

- Document your sales stages and then create a checklist of actions that need to happen at each stage.

4. Negotiation Strategies

Just as I fear that your sales leader won't be providing you with soft skills or discovery training, I'm concerned this will also be true for negotiation training. Whether or not this is the case, I recommend you read or listen to the book *Never Split the Difference: Negotiating As If Your Life*

Depended On It, by Chris Voss. Not only is this book highly entertaining as Voss shares stories about his days with the FBI as their lead international hostage negotiator, but he has also taken all the techniques he learned at the FBI and put them to use negotiating business deals—and even how to purchase a car at the price you want to pay.

Once you've figured out where your negotiation skills training will come from, you next need to sit down with your sales leader to ask the following questions:

- What is the philosophy around discounting at the company?
- Do I have the authority to offer discounts?
- If so, how much leeway do I have and under what circumstances?
- What are the give/gets I should be asking for?
- What other things do we usually negotiate on besides price?
- When do I need to get a leader involved in the negotiation?

You need to understand the company's philosophy on discounting. I've worked for companies that don't ever intend to sell their product at full price and intentionally price it higher than market value so it appears the prospective customer is getting a "great deal" when a 20 percent discount is applied or offered. I've worked with companies that believe in this Kristieism: "Some money is better than no money," so they are willing to negotiate on price rather than lose a deal.

You may be allowed to discount if you get a longer-term agreement or if the quantity reaches a certain level. The point is, you need to understand the philosophy around discounting and what authority you have to negotiate and what will need management approval.

Here's another Kristieism to remember: "Your company will live with the discount you agreed to for the life of the customer." Meaning, it is unlikely that the customer will ever pay full price, *ever*, regardless of price increases that happen over time or at time of renewal.

If your only job is hunting, and you'll never be responsible for contract renewals or selling this customer anything in the future, you might think that discounting is an okay strategy. I'm going to respectfully disagree. Selling on price and not on value is what sales reps do when they don't have the sales skills needed to uncover pain, understand the negative financial impact that pain is having on their organization, or craft a solution that will provide the ROI needed to justify the purchase.

With that said, there are very practical reasons for not discounting. First, discounting will directly reduce your variable income. Most of you who are reading this book are or will be commissioned sales reps. As such, every dollar discounted reduces your take-home pay. Second, the best leads will come from customers referring new business to you. If you are in the habit of downselling your product or service and a customer you discounted refers a prospect to you, you can almost 100 percent guarantee they will have shared what they paid with the company they are referring who will now also expect to pay less for your product or service than it's worth.

I suggest to my clients to never negotiate on price but instead find other "give/gets" to negotiate on, such as payment terms, adding in free professional service hours, or maybe even a free training session for users or administrators. Try to get creative and make sure the prospect is getting value without the need to downsell your product's value.

Homework for Negotiation Strategy:

- Document what your give/gets will be during a negotiation.

---

5. Nurturing Strategies

I just got off the phone with a sales representative I worked with six months ago to close a deal, only to have them, guess what, *do nothing*. We had to close the deal as lost because #stalledisnotastage and moved on.

During this call, the rep said, "You're never going to believe who just called me! The prospect you helped me try to close a while back."

"Ah, yes," I said, "I remember. That one was really disappointing after all the time, energy, and negotiation that went into trying to close the deal with this difficult prospect."

"Yup," he agreed. "So I asked him what he wanted, and he told me that they are opening their offices back up in thirty days and need a workspace management solution ASAP!"

I was super excited to know that all our hard work hadn't been in vain, but I was curious to know how he'd been nurturing the prospect over the past six months. The rep told me he'd been sending the prospect updates on new features as they were rolling out and also mentioned we were going to have a price increase thirty days before the update went into effect. As I had hoped, the rep had been nurturing them in hopes they might come back to life. And they did!

Unfortunately, you will invest time, energy, and negotiation into prospects only to close them as lost, not because they bought from your competitor but because they decided not to buy from anyone at all. In fact, your greatest competition won't come from other companies that sell what you sell. Nope. Your biggest competitor is apathy, the easy path of doing nothing at all.

Of course, apathy isn't the only reason prospects might decide to do nothing; it might be budget or personnel issues or something else, but usually, it's just that they don't have the urgency to invest in solving the problem your product is designed to solve.

That's why it's important for you to have a nurturing strategy in place for lost deals as well as NRN (not right now) prospects. So what do I mean by a *nurturing strategy*? I mean that if you continue to water the seed you planted, it might just grow into a future customer. You need to have a strategy for staying on the prospect's radar so when the problem is big enough that they have to care about it or when they have the budget, your name is the one that comes to mind.

You need to learn if your company has a formal nurturing strategy that's been successful. If not, well, you know what that means: you'll need to put a process in place. I want to caution you that if you hear from your leader that they rely on the marketing department to keep prospects warm, be wary. I do believe marketing should play a part in nurturing prospects, but they should play a *supporting* role. Marketing won't know how far a prospect got down the sales funnel, so they can only provide generic messaging to your former prospects. It's up to you to reach out systematically in a more personalized way, based on your relationship with them.

Also, different types of situations will call for different types of nurture strategies. There should be strategies for prospects you talked to who are qualified and fit your ICP but told you "not right now." These are prospects you didn't get far with, and so they know very little about your company, product, or service.

You'll need a *different* strategy for prospects that went through the entire sales cycle and then decided not to buy. These prospects will be well-educated about your product, but you will need to keep them informed about industry trends, updates to your current product, and new product offerings that may have launched after they walked away.

As an example of how I help reps create a nurturing strategy, I recommend the following:

- Create future tasks in your CRM no less than every three months for each prospect who you either coded as NRN or are closed/lost prospects.

- Friday afternoons are a great time to spend sixty minutes looking around the internet for relevant articles you can share with prospects to help further educate them and set yourself up as a subject matter expert.

- Make sure you're getting updates from product development on new features. It's a good idea to make friends with your Account Management or Customer Success teams because they usually inform customers about updates, and you could the templates they've already produced to inform your past prospects.

The longer you stay at a job, the more likely you are to have the phone ring unexpectedly, like the rep I mentioned earlier who had the prospect from a year ago reach out unexpectedly. And like that rep, it will happen more often if you've been actively nurturing them.

> ## Homework for Nurturing Strategy:
>
> • Determine how you'll nurture your NRNs and your closed/lost prospects.

6. Reputation Strategies

It's getting harder and harder for companies to differentiate themselves from their competition. I recently had a candidate for an Enterprise account executive role ask the founder of a startup I was helping to hire for: "What makes you different from others in the industry?" Unfortunately, the founder struggled to answer the question. I was disappointed but not surprised. There are very few unique offerings and even fewer differentiators between competitors in a given market these days. One of the things that can help set your company apart from others is *you*!

You are, most likely, the first impression a prospect has of your company. How you present yourself is how the prospect will most likely perceive the company you work for. So you need to give careful consideration regarding your personal brand and how it could impact your company's image and your personal success. A strong, personal brand can present you as someone who is an industry expert, a product expert, and a trusted resource.

Where should you start and what decisions do you need to make to create a personal brand and ensure that it's an asset and not a liability? Well, if you took time earlier in the book to determine your sales superpower and pick a swim lane, then you're way ahead of the game. You can take that information and use it to create a personal brand statement. It needs to be short, catchy, and clearly articulate where your expertise lies and how that expertise will benefit their organization or them personally.

Here's an exercise to help you get started. LinkedIn requires a headline of only 200 characters. Take a minute to craft a personal brand statement that will describe you and your area of expertise. Here's one I created for my LinkedIn headline a few years ago:

> *Helping SaaS Startup Founders drive additional top-of-the-funnel to increase revenue through improving people, formalizing and documenting sales processes, and creating a sales accountability culture to ensure success.*

My swim lane is clearly defined: SaaS startup founders.

My areas of expertise are also present: improving people, formalizing and documenting processes, and creating an accountability culture.

The benefit: increased revenue.

Now you take a stab at it.

Once you have your personal branding statement written, you can use it as your north star for developing your overall branding strategy and creating content. You'll want to use the written word, video, and even pictures (use the background picture on your LinkedIn profile to tell them about your passions and expertise) to establish yourself as someone who prospects, customers, coworkers, and even your next boss can see is a true sales professional in your space.

Here are some other things to think about once you've created your branding statement:

- What platforms should you be present on? If you're in B2B sales, LinkedIn is a must, but what about X—are your prospects there? If you're in B2C sales, a presence on Facebook, TikTok, YouTube, and Instagram are probably necessary.
- How will you tell your story? You didn't get to where you are without a little struggle and maybe even help from others. So tell your story to make you more authentic and relatable.

- How often will you post? Writing value-added content is time-consuming, so you need to be realistic about how often you will post. The most important thing is to post consistently.
- Most importantly, add value! Educate your audience and make sure you are offering content that is valuable to them. Remember—you're trying to set yourself apart from the crowd, so if you're just talking about the same thing your competition is talking about in the same way they're talking about it, then you're going to be just like everyone else.

You should reevaluate your personal brand every few years to see if it's still in line with your current superpowers, secret weapon, and swim lane and adjust accordingly.

Homework for Reputation Strategy:

- Create a personal branding statement.

7. Skill-Building Strategies

I feel obligated to ask the following question at some point with every candidate who's going through the interview process with one of my clients: "What formal sales training have you been provided by the previous companies you've worked for?" Unfortunately, I already know the answer, because it's what I hear from almost every candidate . . . *none.*

It seems that unless you have worked for a Fortune 1000 company, you've probably built your sales skills through trial and error, watching YouTube, or listening to Sarah who sits next to you at work. Since most professionals are no longer working in an office full time, you've probably lost one of the best ways to learn—OJT (on-the-job training), better known as eavesdropping—so you may not have even had a "Sarah" sitting next to you.

I'm not sure why companies don't invest the time and money into providing professional sales training, but they don't and because fewer than 100 colleges and universities offer Sales as a major, chances are you're going to have to train yourself.

Setting up a strong skill-building strategy now will allow you to put your growth as a sales professional on "rinse and repeat" because this is how you position yourself as the go-to expert and influencer, not only with prospects but within your company, your community, and your industry.

There are several ways you can get formal sales training to help you with techniques, strategies, and tactics. You can start with taking online courses on LinkedIn Learning, Udemy, and yes, even YouTube. I know several very qualified sales trainers and coaches who are teaching sales online. Here are a few:

- Sales Gravy
- Mike Weinberg
- Winning by Design
- Anthony Iannarino
- Becc Holland
- The Bridge Group
- My Udemy Course "Sales Prospecting Fundamentals: A Complete Guide to Success"

Join sales associations. Associations hold local, regional, and national conferences, and they bring in qualified speakers to train on sales "soft skill" topics, such as Effective Discovery Calls, Prospecting in the Age of AI, Negotiation Skills, etc. If your industry is one with a national, regional, or local association, you should plan to join at least at the local level. This membership will give you access to industry reports and surveys, conferences, and networking events, as well as educational opportunities. It can play an important role in building your reputation and skills as well as getting the inside skinny on the competitor's product so you can not only sell from a more informed position but also offer valuable insights on how your company's product can be improved.

Attend industry conferences. This is not only a great way to invest in your personal knowledge and skills, but it's also a great way to target ideal prospects. Going to national conferences is great but don't overlook local or regional conferences. These smaller events will allow you to rub elbows with prospects and peers in your geographic area. There's a chance prospects in your area are facing different challenges than prospects in other parts of the country because of weather, geography, political climate, or a myriad of other reasons. Having a pulse on what's going on in your backyard could be more important and impactful to your sales success.

As an attendee at a national or regional conference, you can take in the daily keynote speech, which will most likely highlight challenges or trends the industry is facing. The days will also be filled with breakout sessions, allowing you to interact with others on a more personal level. Being an attendee is really a twofer: the opportunity to get face-to-face with your prospects while gaining valuable information.

As an exhibitor at a conference, you can have a booth at the expo. This will give you great exposure to your target audience and let them come to you, as opposed to you having to seek them out. Being an exhibitor isn't the low-cost option; booth space often runs in the thousands, not to mention travel and entertainment costs, but it establishes you as a player in the space and allows you to collect contact information on hundreds of prospects in just a few days.

And there's nothing like a little in-person secret shopping. Whether you're an attendee at the conference or an exhibitor or sponsor, the other great benefit of going to an industry conference is to scope out the competition. All the big players in your space will have a presence at the conference, either as a sponsor, exhibitor, or both. They might also be hosting breakout sessions you can attend to better understand the message they are using to attract prospects. You should also get a look at their product or service offering. Playing industry spy is one of my favorite pastimes at trade shows. I'll circle the competitor's booth like a vulture, making sure to wear non-logo clothes, so I can eavesdrop on conversations the sales reps working the booth are having with passersby. After a couple of days,

I go in for the kill by pretending to be a prospective client. This allows me to ask specific questions to make sure I'm up on their latest product offering, and to fully understand our differentiators.

Attend online seminars, mastermind groups, and workshops. There are several great sales trainers who offer public sales training courses. Some industries have certifications that require annual continuing education credits to stay in compliance. If this is the case, your association membership should have plenty of educational classes to choose from. Taking a class or seminar isn't just a great way to expand your knowledge, it will also allow you to meet others in your industry who may become good resources or network contacts. You never know who could become your next referral partner, mentor, or industry advocate.

Read sales books. There are so many great books (in addition to the one you're reading). A quick internet search can guide you to sales books specific to your needs. The more you invest in reading and listening to other experts, joining associations and networking groups, having a presence at their events (live and online), developing meaningful relationships with mentors, colleagues, and referral partners, and giving informed suggestions to your product development team, the more exponential your rise to Rock Star status will become.

Listen to podcasts. There are so many good sales and business podcasts out there. Test drive a few to see which host's style best fits your personality and needs.

Engage with mentors. Hopefully you have people in your inner sales circle who have been in sales longer than you have and who may have something to offer by way of 1:1 coaching. Attending industry conferences can also be a great way to find a mentor. What better place to "interview" prospective mentors than a conference filled with industry experts, some of whom have probably sold into your industry in the past. It's important for you to have a small circle of people you can turn to for advice, help, and introductions, and having someone who really knows the ins and outs of your industry can come in handy as you navigate the rough waters of trying to wrap your arms around a new industry.

When I was in the elearning industry, I met a man, Edwin, who turned out to be not only a great friend, but also a mentor I leaned on for years. He was my point of contact for a vendor we partnered with, and he'd been in the industry two and a half years longer than I had, so I was constantly calling him with questions and picking his brain about everything from the industry and competitors to leading and managing people. He was someone I could lean on when things weren't going well and I needed a pep talk. Because our companies were partners, I also enjoyed strategizing with him on pricing, sales strategy, and compensation plans for my reps. He really was a one-stop shop for information and support, and if I needed a drinking buddy, he was good for that too!

Join a networking or mastermind group. Another good place to build your reputation, find a mentor, and meet prospects and referral partners is networking events or online industry groups. Push yourself to attend at least one meetup or networking event quarterly. Most networking events will have some type of panel or fireside chat presentation on a hot industry topic with experts in your industry. Attending these types of events will give you an opportunity to hear from subject matter experts, which will allow you to evaluate possible mentors before you decide to approach them. And as you develop your reputation in the industry, having participated frequently from the audience puts you in a great position to apply to speak or appear on a panel.

I wish that every organization understood the importance and ROI that providing professional sales training to their team could have on the company's revenue and each individual's earnings, but alas, I hear too many times from candidates that the answer to my question about having been provided professional sales training is a hard *no*!

Homework for Skill-building Strategy:

- Follow industry experts and groups on social media.
- Listen to podcasts.
- Read trade publications.
- Join your industry's national association and get active in your local chapter.
- Attend regional and national industry conferences.
- Find a mentor.
- Join a networking or mastermind group.

15

Know Your Tools

"Sales Enablement Tools aren't a punishment, they're a gift from your company."

It's easy to get excited about sales tools. But anything that doesn't serve a purpose is a distraction. So I don't want reps to get caught up in how to use all the tech that might be available just because it exists.

That said, sales tools have come a long way since I started my first sales leadership gig back in 2000. Back then, we only had a CRM system to work with. No "tech stack," no gamification software, and the term "sales enablement" wasn't coming out of anyone's mouth.

The swing from manual to automated has been swift over the past ten years. With hundreds of tools to help you work faster, smarter, and better, you can get lost in the tools abyss. Here, we're going to break down the types of tools available and what you really need to be successful day-to-day. Then you can build your knowledge base of what tools are already in place, which ones belong on your "must get" list, and which tools go on the wish list for later.

CRM Tools

The CRM (customer relationship management) system is the center of the sales tools universe and, as most of us say, the "single source of truth." All other sales software tools will integrate into your CRM so all the data you need to make decisions is in one place. This is a must-have tool in your sales toolbox. I hear reps complaining about how much time it takes to document everything in the CRM system, and it almost sounds like they think the company has purchased a CRM system to make their job harder when, if you use it properly, it actually will make your job and life easier *and* add to your commission checks.

This software tool is used by companies across the world to help track and manage all prospect and customer activities that happen on a day-to-day basis, including email, calls, text messages, direct mail, and other "touches." Basically, your CRM system is just one big database of information about companies and contacts.

Your CRM system is definitely the first place you should go when looking for your ideal customer profile. If you're selling B2C, it should contain demographic information. If you're selling B2B, it should contain firmographic information about each company that has been a customer up to the present. This information will allow you to build a list based on some of the ICP information we discussed in the last chapter. That's the good news.

But like anything where data is pulled from a variety of sources by humans and put in one centralized place, also by humans, the downside is that good data goes bad, and it goes bad at a rapid rate. Think about the number of people who lost their jobs in 2020 or quit during the "Great Resignation" of 2021. Any of those people who were in your database as a contact or decision-maker just increased its "dirty" factor. Current thinking says the data in your CRM is bad eighteen months after you've put it in, and with these recent shifts, I think that number is optimistic.

It's not just bad data you have to worry about, it's also incomplete data. Missing or inaccurate phone numbers, email addresses, and job titles will cause you frustration as you use your CRM to build your ICP and prospect list.

Here's where I beg you to be part of the solution and not the dirty data problem. As you're working in your CRM and you find missing or bad data that you can update, please "just do it!" If everyone who works in the CRM takes action to own the data they're working with, the data will stay cleaner longer. Okay, off my soapbox about dirty data—for now anyway. Later we'll talk about CRM management as one of the actions in your sales process.

Many sales reps think keeping the CRM up to date is admin work and sales leaders make them do it just to torture them. In actuality, a healthy CRM should be listed alongside other benefits, such as health insurance, PTO, and tuition reimbursement, because it really should be that important to you. As you start your career at a company and begin to prospect, you might make fifty calls a day and talk to five contacts a day. There is *no way* you'll remember those conversations even four days later, and there is also no way anyone but you will know what information is going to be important for the next contact with the prospect and therefore needs to be entered into the CRM. Keeping your "single point of truth" up to the minute isn't a job for admin; it's a gift you give your future self.

Here's the truth: the CRM is your friend and will make you look really smart when a prospect you spoke with three months ago calls out of the blue and says, "Hi, this is Sally Smith from ABC Enterprise. I'm sure you won't remember, but we spoke three months ago." As soon as she says her name, you type the information into your CRM, and, lo and behold, there are the notes from your call three months ago. "Of course, Sally," you say. "You were just about to go on maternity leave and wanted to reconnect after you came back to work. I hope you and the baby are doing well!" Can you imagine the look on Sally's face? But that's exactly how professional sales reps use the CRM to their advantage.

So put CRM on your "must use" list and learn all that you can about the one you have available to you.

Automation Tools

Another category you should consider when building out your sales toolbox is automation tools. The hardest sales activity is prospecting because it truly is a numbers game, and even though you're playing the odds, the success rate is still low. Sending emails no one replies to, leaving voicemails that aren't returned, having connection requisitions on LinkedIn ignored, and when you *do* get someone who answers the phone, hearing, "We're happy with our current vendor" can be heartbreaking.

Sales is a rejection-filled sport, but the highest rejection comes from outbound prospecting. Using a manual process to do outbound prospecting is inefficient, and when you have a good automation tool that can track and manage the process for you, also unnecessary. These tools, when used intelligently and strategically, can put outbound prospecting on autopilot so you can focus on the quality of the conversation when a prospect does answer the phone!

Some CRM systems, like HubSpot and Pipedrive, have prospecting automation built in. Others, like Salesforce, integrate with tools such as Salesloft, Outreach.io, Groove, and Apollo to allow you to create an outbound workflow that will make your life easier.

Once you've made decisions about the actions in your sales process, you'll find software platforms that allow you to determine how many times you'd like to touch a prospect, the type of communication method you'd like to use for each touch, and what to do next based on interest level will uplevel your ability to "work smarter, not harder." This paves the way for you to pay more attention to the details that give your Rock Star sales strategy a push in the right direction.

Data Clean-Up Tools

As we discussed earlier, dirty data is real and really frustrating. There are several software companies that can not only help you find clean data, but that can also help you clean up your dirty database and eliminate contacts who are no longer with the company and replace them with legitimate contacts. They can also help you add missing data to your database, such as cell phone numbers and email addresses. These tools or services may not be relevant if the CRM you'll be inheriting hasn't gotten much use, but if it's chockfull of data collected by multiple reps over several years and hasn't been audited or cleaned for some time, this step can save you hours of misdirected efforts as well as the embarrassment and missed opportunities of acting on outdated information.

Analytics Tools

Remember what I said about prospecting being a numbers game? When you're reaching out to large numbers of contacts, you'll want to get reliable data to make better decisions around what's working and what's not. Most CRM systems, once they've been cleaned up and maintained as a quality source of truth, will have reports and dashboards you can build to provide analytics. You'll learn things like which emails—or really, which subject lines—are getting the most attention, how many calls you need to make before someone will answer the phone (current data says a 7 percent connect rate is average), and how many touches you need to make before a prospect moves from awareness to interest.

These tools can also be constructed to tell you important pipeline information, which will help you do your personal sales math so you can figure out exactly the number and type of deals you need to add to the pipeline to ensure you hit your quota: things like your average sale, close rate, the number of days it takes you to close a deal, the reason deals are not closing, and much more. If your CRM isn't tracking all the information you think you need, there are other tools, such as Tableau, Gong, Sisense, and Qlik Sense that will provide you with more advanced analytics as well as integrate with your CRM to give you more advanced data. I usually refer to these as "business intelligence (BI) tools."

Meeting Schedulers

A meeting scheduler, such as Calendly or Chili Piper, lets you preemptively manage the times you're available for different types of meetings, then generates a link you can send to prospects and clients so they can book into a time slot that works for them. This saves time and frustration for you and the other person because there's no going back and forth on best times to meet. It should also automate your meeting reminders so the other person is getting emails and/or texts to remind them of the time and location of the meeting that was scheduled.

Conversation Intelligence Tools

You know conversations can signal empathy and credibility, build trust, and make prospects feel comfortable talking to you, or they can do just the opposite. Conversation intelligence tools record, transcribe, and analyze your sales calls to help you identify key words and topics so you can recognize and repeat patterns that work and avoid those that don't. Tools such as Gong, Chorus, Balto, and Fathom help you get the call coaching you need to improve your sales skills and help you be a more effective communicator over the phone.

Electronic Signature Software

If you've signed a document online for any reason, you know how convenient and easy it is. No more printing, scanning and then emailing back contracts or agreements. This software isn't just more convenient for you as a rep, but also more convenient for the signer. A good tool in this category will also provide a high level of digital security, notify all parties when a document has been signed, and provide a link for all parties to view or download the document. Ideally, use of an electronic signature tool should provide convenience, security, efficiency, and quality documentation.

There may be other tools already in place, or in some specialized industries, other tools that you'll want to add to your "tool belt." But the key is that you know what tools are available to you and which ones you want to add as soon as possible.

LinkedIn

LinkedIn is one of the most important and powerful business tools you should be leveraging. From creating a powerful profile that screams "subject matter expert" to following influencers in your industry and profession, LinkedIn and LinkedIn Sales Navigator, when used effectively, can help you look like the Rock Star you are while reducing the time you spend researching prospects and trying to figure out what's important to them. I'm not a LinkedIn expert, but my friend Brynne Tillman is, so if you want to make sure you're getting your money's worth out of LinkedIn or LinkedIn Sales Navigator, sign up for one of the many classes she offers.

Artificial Intelligence

AI (artificial intelligence) is the newest kid on the block. ChatGPT rocketed on the scene in 2023 with a vengeance and brought with it a lot of questions from the sales industry regarding how to use it, when to use it, how much to use it, and if it will eventually replace sales professionals.

As of this publication, I'd say the sales professionals I'm working with are AI-curious but also suspicious. I've been using it mostly to research topics, companies, and contacts I'm prospecting. I've found it to be a time-saver and mostly helpful, and sometimes it even provides a different point of view.

With so much unchartered at this point, based on the technology available at the time of this writing, let me share my thoughts around when you should consider using AI:

- You should use it to help you do pre-call planning.
- You should use it to help you understand things, such as:
  » A day in the life of your buyer
  » Industry trends for the industries you sell into
  » Competitors and their differentiators.
- You should use it to help you do repetitive tasks more efficiently.
- You can use it to help you edit an email or shorten one before you send to a prospect or customers.

- It can crunch your personal sales math numbers to help you iden-tify areas you could improve.
- You can use it for sales coaching.
- It will help you better understanding the market conditions and pricing.
- Use it for post-call note-taking.

Here's what I don't think it should be used for:
- Writing an email from scratch to a prospect or customer.
- Automating AI-generated voice calls for cold-calling.
- Telling you what to charge someone.
- Making a human connection.

Homework for Knowing Your Tools:

- Figure out which tools your company is providing and make sure you are properly trained so you're getting the most out of these tools.
- Understand the quality of the information within the tools so you know how much you can rely on their data.
- Make a list of tools not currently available and categorize them as must have, nice to have, or fun to have someday.
- Determine how you'll use AI within your sales processes.

At this point, you should have compiled a foundation of information and intelligence about your current sales position. You'll use this frame-work with any new employer, product, or service to build a comprehen-sive knowledge base. I also recommend you revisit this framework period-ically, just to see if your initial research was valid and to make sure you're not building a process on a false premise or outdated information.

Once you've done your due diligence to gather the information required to build your Rock Star sales process, it's time to make some decisions. You're ready to put that information to use, make decisions about the actions you will take, and start selling your way into the life you want to have!

16

Process, Planning, and Prospects— Decisions and Actions

I once worked for a CFO who regularly said, "That sounds like a broken process."

I got tired of hearing it, not because he was wrong, but because he was right. Now I'm the one who regularly says the process is broken, and people may get tired of hearing it, but they soon realize just how true it is. I'm not sure a broken process is better than no process at all, so I want to make sure you have a formal and repeatable sales process you can rely on.

Dean, who you may remember was my boss, mentor, and number one cheerleader, loved to use the phrase, "Stop using the 'Fire, Fire, Fire, Aim' strategy." That was his way of making a rep aware that they were working without a formal plan in place and shooting from the hip.

We need to avoid falling into that trap because it's a terrible waste of time and ammunition, not to mention there's a risk of friendly fire damage. You need to make sure you're prepared to show up as the professional salesperson you are. You never want to give the impression that you're figuring it out as you're going along, and you don't want to be faking it, just hoping to make it before anyone notices you're flying by the seat of your pants. When you engage prospects or clients before you have a plan and a formal process in place, that's exactly what you're doing—flying by the seat of your pants.

Being successful in sales requires knowing where you want to be and a process and plan for getting there. It will be almost impossible for you to sell your way into a better and more financially rewarding situation if you don't have formal and repeatable sales processes you can rely on.

I often get calls from founders or sales leaders asking if I will come in and evaluate their sales reps because they aren't sure they have the right players on the team. I tell them, gently, that I'd be happy to interview each rep and provide feedback, but only after I've had a chance to evaluate their sales process. Most of the time, I find the people aren't broken, but the sales process is. If there is no successful and formalized sales process, a set of Key Performance Indicators (KPIs), or a compensation structure that drives the right behavior, then I know the team has been set up to fail.

Because my swim lane is working with early-stage clients, I often run into sales teams that are trying to drive revenue with little to no process or a badly broken process, and absolutely no documentation of their process at all. But it certainly happens in mature companies as well. I don't want this to be you, so let's discuss how, even if your company has some processes in place, you can make them your own—or better yet, help your organization improve their existing processes.

The Top of the Sales Funnel–Prospecting, Discovery, and Your Sales Cycle

There are two primary sales activities you need to make sure you have a plan and a formal process for: 1. adding prospects to your pipeline and 2. moving those prospects through the pipeline. So let's start at the top of the sales funnel with the decisions you'll need to make about your prospecting strategy.

Having a full pipeline is the starting point for your success. As I've mentioned earlier in the book, an anemic pipeline will cause panic, which in turn will cause bad decisions. So I want to make sure you understand the many ways you could go about building a pipeline filled with true ideal prospects and not imposters.

There are a variety of ways to add new leads into your pipeline. Three of the primary sources are inbound marketing leads, SDRs doing outbound prospecting, and self-sourced leads sourced by *you*. If your company has its act together and is working smarter, there will be a referral strategy in place, which we'll cover in Chapter 20.

I believe filling the sales funnel *should* be a team sport with sales and marketing working together. In fact, I'd really like the marketing department to be called the Lead Generation Department, but if that isn't the case at your company yet I want to arm you with strategies that will ensure your pipeline is full. Then you can hit your personal sales goal consistently, even *without* support from the marketing department.

When you collected information about your company's prospecting strategy, you should have learned as much as possible about which lead sources produced the highest close rate. Once you understand which type of prospects will be easiest to close, you should then take your strengths and secret weapons into consideration. Do you connect with people better in person, or do you love smiling and dialing for dollars? Do you like to warm them up with an email before calling or dropping in on a prospect in person?

You need to put a personal prospecting process in place that will make your time spent prospecting fruitful. You're looking for *quality* not quantity, so make sure you understand how best to find qualified prospects who might be interested in becoming future customers.

Once you have made decisions about the methods you will employ to find prospects, you need to make decisions about how you will qualify them and then move them through your sales pipeline.

Here's how I define a qualified prospect: *a person or company that has a problem they need/want to fix, which your product or service can solve, and who is willing to spend money in the near future to solve that problem.*

Obviously, chasing unqualified prospects is a waste of your time and theirs, so let's discuss how to properly qualify a prospect.

The key to qualifying a prospect is doing a proper discovery call or meeting. The discovery call is about listening and learning, not selling. Because until you've qualified them, you can't possibly know what to sell them, how to sell to them, or even if you should be selling to them at all.

The Kristieism that comes into play here is this: "It has to be all about them before it can be all about you, and before it can be all about us." That means the discovery conversation isn't the time to talk about you, your company, or your product. Your time will come, but right now, it's all about them.

There are a few reasons why you need to focus on them and not on you:

- No one will care about you, your product, or your company until they know you care about them—meaning, you need to earn the right to hear their struggles, by listening and caring, and then you can become a trusted advisor.

- How can you determine if they truly are a qualified prospect if you don't spend time to understand their issues and how those issues are impacting their business financially? You need to thoroughly understand what's broken, what they've tried in the past to fix what's broken, and if they are really willing to devote time, money, and resources to fix what's broken. Remember, wasting your time and theirs is just that—a waste.

- Discovery allows you to build a relationship and the trust you will need throughout the sales cycle. People want to trust those they are doing business with.

I describe the discovery call this way: You're the doctor, and the prospect is the patient. You need to ask enough questions to come up with a diagnosis. Sometimes, the doctor can't find anything wrong, and other times, what they find can't be fixed or at least fixed by them. So make sure that your solution can fix what's wrong; I'll call this *fit*. If there isn't fit, a professional sales rep needs to be honest about that and recommend another solution or idea that might be more helpful.

A good discovery meeting isn't over until you can answer these questions:

- What's their current situation?
- What issues are they having with the current situation?
- What is the financial impact each issue is having on the organization?
- What have they tried in the past to resolve the issue?
- Why didn't that work?
- What's their dream outcome?
- Who else will be involved with this project/decision?
- When would they like to fix the issue?
- Are they willing to pay to fix the issue?
- Are they willing to put another *firm* meeting on the calendar in the next two weeks?

Once you have gathered that information, you should be able to "diagnose" their problem and determine if you can solve it and if they are really interested in solving it. If yes, then you have a fit. Then, and only then, do I recommend you put your prospect into the pipeline.

I don't put a prospect into an active pipeline until I've done a discovery call and determined there is a fit—by the way, that's *my* recommendation; every company works a little differently, so be flexible here. If you decide to put a prospect into your active pipeline without the discovery call, make sure you've added a notation or tag (I'll share more about managing this part of your process later) so you can identify prospects where fit has been determined, as well as those with whom you have not yet had a discovery meeting.

Once the prospect has agreed to further evaluate your solution, you need to have a process for managing the sales cycle. Here are the things you need to consider while building out this process:

- How will you track sales stages as you move prospects through the sales cycle? I like to have four to five stages, not including Closed/Won and Closed/Lost. Here are the ones I most commonly use:
1. Fit Identified

2. Product/Solution Fit Identified
3. Verbal Agreement
4. Negotiation
5. Contract Agreement

Then, of course, Closed/Won and Closed/Lost.

- What will the criteria be for moving from one stage to another?
- How long should the prospect stay in each stage before they start to fall into the "Stalled deal" category?
- How will I ensure the prospect is continuously moving forward in the process?
- What criteria will I use to move them to Closed/Lost (i.e., my walkaway point)?

You also need to decide how you'll handle different situations that might arise throughout the sales cycle. After years of coaching sales reps and doing pipeline reviews, here's some advice about managing your pipeline and sales cycle: do not let your prospect take control of the sales cycle! You need to remain in control throughout the cycle. How do you do this? Here are some best practices:

Firm it up. End every meeting/call with agreed upon next steps and a firm follow-up call/meeting scheduled on the calendar. Don't let your prospect tell you, "Oh, just give me a call next week" or "I'll call you after we've talked." You don't want to be chasing down your prospects after they didn't do what they said they would.

Hold your prospects accountable. You need to understand how to hold your prospect accountable and assign homework. Holding them accountable means making sure that they hit deadlines for getting back to you, sending you information you might need, etc.

The best way to do this is to ask, "How long do you think it will take you to pull that together? Great, so let's get a firm call on the calendar for next Tuesday."

Be prepared. If a deal is going to stall, it will normally happen during stages three or four. This is when your prospect will say something like, "We need to discuss internally," or "We need to evaluate other options/vendors." You still need to have a firm follow-up call on the calendar, even if it's just for ten minutes to get a progress update.

Stick to reality. It's a short trip from a fantasy funnel to a quota nightmare. Hope is not a good sales strategy, and a "fantasy funnel" doesn't help anyone, least of all you. Be real about where each prospect is in the funnel and which prospects are not really in the funnel except in your dreams.

Move 'em forward or move 'em out. Stalled is *not* a sales stage. You need to have a process for handling deals that have stalled out or prospects who are ghosting you. Decide your walkaway point now so you know how many times you are willing to attempt to connect with them before sending them the Dear Jane/John email and closing them as lost.

Keep your CRM "lean and clean." There's nothing that will cost you more than sloppy note-taking or "dirty data." Your CRM is your single source of truth. If it isn't in there, it didn't "officially" happen, and if it is in there, it had better be true and current. So do yourself a huge favor and make a regular discipline of updating your CRM. That means good note-taking too. If you spoke to someone on the phone, met with them in person, or ran into them at a tradeshow, then your next step is to record the interaction in your CRM with notes regarding the conversation and the outcome of that conversation. There's nothing more embarrassing than reaching out to someone in your CRM system that you think, based on the information you're seeing, hasn't had any interaction with your company in months, only to learn that coworker Carol just spoke with them yesterday and didn't bother to put her notes in the system. Thanks, Carol! I tell reps that anyone in the company should be able to go into the CRM system, pull up a company or contact, and know exactly what is going on with that prospect or customer.

Be Prepared to Face Your Greatest Competition: Apathy

Your discovery process should have prepared you to nail the next two phases in moving the prospect through your pipeline. First, you need to demonstrate exactly where your solution matches their problem by focusing on *their* perception of the problem, not yours. And second, you need to show them, in detail, the cost of no agreement.

You know the cost of no agreement for you, right? No sale, no client, no commission. But does the *client* understand the cost of no agreement for them? If you've been doing continual discovery, *you* know what it's going to cost them if you can't reach an agreement and move the sale forward. It's going to cost them time, safety risks, security risks, and so on, but all of those costs have financial implications, so bottom line, it's going to cost them money.

Remember the story I told you about the prospect that came back after six months because the sales rep had a nurturing strategy in place? For most reps, that isn't what usually happens. What happens most often is you lose your prospect because they decided to do *nothing*, and they don't come back after six months, or twelve months, or at all. This is the most frustrating way to lose a deal. You've done your job. You did the discovery, uncovered the problems they have, got them to acknowledge that it's an issue costing them time and money, and they agreed they need to make a change, yet they end up doing nothing. And the reason they're doing nothing is because you haven't given them reason enough to move. They're stuck in apathy, and you're stuck with a prospect you could help but a deal you can't close.

Let's dig a little deeper here since this will bite you in the backside more times than you will be happy about. There are a few reasons a prospect won't care enough to make the decision to buy.

- The price of the solution is greater than the cost of the issue.
- There isn't budget at this point to solve the issue.
- Change is hard, and they don't have any internal change management process.

Assuming that your prospect is a decision-maker who can "write the check," figuratively speaking, or authorize the necessary resources to make the purchase, the bottom line in each of those cases is the prospect didn't see enough value in your solution to build an internal business case to invest time, money, and resources into solving the issue.

Understanding each of these scenarios will allow you to quickly move your prospect past the sticking point or move them out of your pipeline completely, so let's examine each of them more fully.

First, there is no reason for anyone to spend money on a solution that is more costly than the issue at hand. It's important that you not only understand the pain the company has but also the financial impact that pain is costing the organization. Financial pain normally manifests itself in two ways: low revenue or high overhead. It's important that after you've built some trust, but before you get too far down the sales cycle, you address the true cost of this pain to the company's bottom line. This is where you will learn if the cost to solve it will make financial sense based on the cost of the issue. I call this "computing the cost of no agreement."

I like to ask the question this way: "What do you think not solving the issue is costing your organization annually?" If the cost of not solving it is less than the cost of your product or service, then you don't have "fit." The sooner you can determine this, the less time you will waste on a bad-fit prospect.

Sometimes there truly aren't funds available to purchase your product. With that said, if the issue is great enough and you've done a good job of building value, money will usually "appear" from somewhere. I like to ask the question this way: "Is this a budgeted initiative?" If they say yes, then you need to ask if the budget is sufficient to cover the cost of your product or service. If they say no, then ask this question: "How are non-budgeted purchases handled at your company?" If they really don't have funds, then you need to understand when/if that might change and schedule a call closer to that time period.

It's important that you #ownyourownshit with regard to the prospect not seeing enough value in your product. If this is the case, you need to go back to the beginning and resell the prospect, not on features, but on benefits. I think one of the worst benefits sales reps use to sell is the "It will save you time" benefit. This is the least effective pain that you can solve, and usually, when it gets to the decision-maker, they will shoot down the idea since it's not *their* time that's being used inefficiently. Time is money. Find out the financial cost of time lost and show them the figures.

Another reason that prospects might do nothing is psychological—change is hard, regardless if it's good or bad change. You can cut this off at the pass earlier in the sales cycle to help reduce the risk of being blindsided by this. I like to open up the topic this way: "Ms. Prospect, tell me about the last time you switched vendors or added a new vendor to the mix." I'm trying to understand if they have a change management process in place and whether that recent change in vendors, and probably their process as a result, was a positive or negative experience. No employee really likes to have to learn a new process, even if it benefits them, but it's much easier if the company has a successful strategy for rolling out new vendors or solutions company-wide.

I've worked with companies that lost one too many deals to "change is hard" objections, and as a result, they put together a rollout playbook complete with email templates to send to employees, explaining why the change is being made and communicate suggestions to the departments most impacted by the change. Sometimes you'll have to take the initiative to work with your prospect to put a successful rollout plan in place so when they go to ask for the money, they're prepared to answer the question, "How are we going to successfully roll this new vendor's product out to the company?"

Again, make sure the person you're trying to move out of apathy is a person whose ability to care about the solution is likely to result in a sale. According to Gartner, there are between seven and ten decision-makers for a purchase. If you only have one point of contact, you are at a disadvantage. Spending too much time with low-level contacts without getting higher level contacts involved is usually a waste of your time. I know everyone says they have buying authority, but few really do.

Titles are cheap, and they can be deceptive. If your point of contact is too far down the food chain from the decision-maker to have influence, or as I like to say, "To have a checkbook," getting them to care about the solution won't close the deal. You need to find out if you're trying to sell to someone who not only doesn't sit with the Knights of the Round Table (also known as the executives in the boardroom) but who doesn't even know where the round table is located. I like to ask the question this way: "Who else will be involved in this decision?" When you have the answer, your next step is to connect with those people, pronto.

Now that we understand what apathy objections we might bump up against as we're working the funnel, let's discuss how we should address objections that will present themselves throughout the sales cycle.

I teach the best way to handle objections is by asking questions to better seek to understand. For each objection you think you might receive from a prospect, make sure you have written two or three questions you would want to ask to be sure you have fully fleshed out the objection and can speak to the issue they've surfaced in a way that will address their concerns.

As an example, I worked with a company a while back that had yet to build an app for their software platform. Other competitors in the space were offering one, and even though their overall platform was more robust than their competitors, the lack of an app was a sticking point for some prospects. I worked with the sales team to come up with a few questions to better flesh out if not having an app was a deal-breaker for the prospect or if it was just a "nice to have."

Feature deal-breakers are hard to overcome but not impossible, and the best way to address a product or service shortfall is to hit it head on. In his book *Never Split the Difference*, ex-FBI negotiator Chris Voss explains a technique he calls an "Accusation Audit." The idea is to preemptively and offensively deal with any objections you think may be coming and address them before the prospect verbalizes them.

For example, "I know you might be thinking that our competitors have more reports than we do so how can we be charging the same amount with fewer reports?" You know the objection is coming because you've heard it before, so waiting until the prospect brings it up puts you on the defensive. Be proactive and bring up the lack of a feature you think will be important to your prospect before they are forced to address it with you. This saves you from being put on the defensive and helps build trust.

When negotiations are happening with the client's full understanding of the match between their problems and your solution and the cost of not reaching an agreement, most of the objections have already been handled. Then, if you need to find a way to meet in the middle on price, you can look at ways to modify the deliverables to match their budget.

The most important processes and plans for consistent success will be how you fill the top of the funnel and how you move those prospects through the sales cycle from discovery to closed/won or closed/lost. Make sure your decisions are dialed in, then create your action plan so it becomes part of your mental memory. Then you can focus your critical-thinking skills on strategies for the deals in your pipeline most likely to close.

Homework for Setting Up Your Personal Prospecting, Discovery, and Sales Cycle Process:

- Determine a personal prospecting strategy that will play to your strengths.
- Determine criteria for moving a prospect from one stage of the sales cycle to the next stage.
- Decide how long a prospect should stay in each stage before they start to fall into the "Stalled" category.
- Determine how you will ensure the prospect is continuously moving forward in the process.
- Create formal criteria for when you'll send the Dear Jane/John email and walk away.
- Determine how you'll hold your prospects accountable.

Honesty Is the Best Process: Your Negotiation and Nurturing Processes

Remember the client who originally offered me a position as their fulltime VP of Sales before I decided consulting was the next right step-change for me?

While interviewing, the owner proudly told me they had over $5M in the pipeline. "Wow!" I said. "That's great! Everyone needs five times the quota, but very few teams actually have that. Especially when you only have two account executives."

"Yes, we've worked hard," said the owner.

When they accepted my offer to become their Fractional VP of Sales instead of their employee, I soon found myself at the conference table with their two AEs, one SDR, and the owner for our first pipeline review meeting.

I was excited. They had $5M in the pipeline, and I couldn't wait to see how many deals were in each stage, how large each deal was, and to determine how much we could realistically close this quarter. I was seeing some big numbers in my mind and looked forward to knocking their socks off by setting some high quotas and proving we could meet them.

As each of the AEs presented their pipelines, my Spidey sense started to sound the alarm. Each of their pipelines barely crossed the $1M mark. Where was the other $3M I had been told existed? I reluctantly posed the question, "I thought there was five million dollars in the pipeline. Where's the other three million?"

"Oh," said the owner, "it's in the Stalled stage!"

"Stalled stage?" I asked, borrowing the mirroring technique straight out of one of my favorite books, *Never Split the Difference* by Chris Voss and biting my tongue to keep from yelling, "Stalled is *not* a stage!"

"Yes, that's where we put all our deals that are stalled out but that will close eventually."

My brain was spinning. They had 60 percent less in the pipeline than I had been led to believe, but that wasn't the scary part. The scary thing was that that $3M in the pipeline . . .

1. was cold and getting colder by the minute;

2. had deals in it that had entered the Bermuda Triangle Sales stage over two years ago; and,

3. they actually believed it was okay to count that $3M as an active pipeline.

Once I got over the feeling of having been the victim of a classic bait and switch, I realized this type of thinking was going to be job security for me as a consultant. Because, as I learned over the next several years, they were not the only company who secretly or not so secretly kept a list of "Stalled" deals.

This Fantasy Funnel they had created was very dangerous. It allowed them to think things were better than they were, gave them false hope, and could easily have caused them to make bad financial decisions. But most importantly, it kept them from doing what they really needed to do to have $5M of active deals in their pipeline.

The person you lie to most often, not surprisingly, is yourself. That client wasn't lying to me; they were lying to themselves and each other. But Rock Stars can't afford to lie to themselves, and they aren't afraid to be honest with themselves either. Your sales process needs to have built-in "truth meters" for what's really going on so you avoid traps, like thinking you have to discount your price to win deals, buying into your own "fantasy funnels," or thinking your toughest competition is the other company.

Getting honest with yourself will be tough, but if you make decisions and establish criteria for your negotiation and nurturing strategies before you start building your sales funnel, your life will be a whole lot easier, and your paychecks will get a whole lot beefier.

Let's start with negotiations. I wish I could tell you how many times I've been told, "We had to give them a discount, or we would have lost that deal," but I can't because I've lost count. I will say that, in at least 95 percent of those cases, they didn't have to give a discount to avoid losing the sale; they had to give a discount because they hadn't been diligent in creating and following a process to build value for their product or service.

This is exactly why I say, "Discovery is not an event; it's a process." The negotiation process should actually be a *continuation* of the discovery process. In the discovery call, you're learning about a prospect's needs, values, and readiness to make a purchase decision to determine fit. But once you've determined fit, you must continue to learn about their needs, values, and readiness to buy if you want to avoid being backed into the "lose money or lose the sale" corner.

The negotiation process is never based on price; it's always based on trust. If every time you have a conversation with the prospect, you're focused on pitching and presenting, and you're not continually doing discovery, you're missing opportunities to prepare for a successful negotiation. But if you're naturally curious during discovery and building trust throughout the sales cycle by asking good questions, listening, and responding to their answers, and providing quality information and insights, you're going to increase trust as time goes on. As trust increases, your prospect is likely to share more details, and reveal more information with every conversation you have.

That means that by the time you need to negotiate price, you should know a lot more about their needs, their priorities, the problems this purchase will solve for them, and what it will cost them to choose a different solution or no solution at all.

When you're being honest and #owningyourownshit, you'll find negotiations are fewer, easier, and faster with fewer discounts than you thought possible.

So let's talk about how honesty as a process can help you create a nurturing process. Just as your negotiation process is really a continuation of your discovery process, your nurturing process is really a continuation of your sales cycle. The decisions you need to make about this process will depend on a number of factors, and if you're not living in reality about where your prospects are in the cycle, how many touches it takes to move them through the cycle, and when they're no longer an active, qualified lead, you're going to get these factors wrong.

When you first begin to fill your sales funnel, it will be tempting to consider every lead a prospect. That's how those fantasy funnels happen. But what you consider your prospecting list, I would probably refer to as the "maybe pile." Maybe they have an issue they want to solve. Maybe they will be interested in what you sell. Maybe they will even buy. Maybe they should be interested and aren't. Or maybe they aren't in a position to buy right now. Some of those maybes may be prospects, but most of them aren't.

This is the perfect time to help you understand my philosophy around suspects versus prospects. Just because a company fits your ICP, it doesn't automatically make them a prospect. Until you've spoken to a decision-maker or influencer and qualified them based on their awareness of having an issue that needs solving and their willingness to spend money to solve it, they're a suspect. Prospects stay in your sales cycle. Suspects go into your nurturing process.

Here's a visualization that will help you understand why you want your sales funnel to contain *only* prospects. Imagine you have a stack of paper. It is 8 1/2 x 11 x 4 inches tall. Now imagine that to move each piece of paper into the stack labeled "Closed/Won," you must touch, read, and evaluate each one of those sheets of paper every week, even every two weeks.

You're probably going to skimp on those touches—get through half the pile and go home, skim the information, and generally fail to give the proper attention to some of the most important pieces of paper. So it's inevitable that some of the best prospects in the stack will get lost in the shuffle. The implications of this kind of process are obvious. You're working harder, not smarter; you're spending time touching pieces of paper that will never move into the next stage while neglecting pages that would move quickly if they only got the proper attention.

So, now picture you're going to sort that stack of papers into two piles: a Yes pile and a No pile. Let's get started.

The way prospects get into the Yes pile is easy—you connect with them, and they acknowledge they have an issue and are willing to spend money to fix their issue, *and* they are willing to speak again to see if your solution could fix the issue. These go into your sales cycle and stay there until they are Closed/Won or stop moving forward.

Your No pile is every bit as important as your Yes pile. There are two paths into your No pile. One path is obvious—you connect with them, and they tell you No or Not Right Now, which is a No until something changes.

The second way prospect end up in the No pile is to do nothing. They never answer the phone when you call, never reply to an email you send, and never accept a LinkedIn connection request or InMail. In short, they "submarine" on you, diving so deep you can't locate them. Or maybe they continue to respond, but they refuse to be accountable and follow through. They don't keep appointments; they haven't done what they said they would do, or they haven't talked to whom they promised to talk to. The lead seems to have "stalled," but we both know "Stalled" is not a stage in your sales cycle. Stalled is either a No or a Not Right Now, and it's your job to figure out which.

Until you sort that stack of papers, you don't know which are Nos, which are Maybes, and which are Yeses just waiting to happen. It's your job to play amateur detective and uncover clues to help you determine if a prospect is masquerading as a suspect but is really a prospect in disguise or if you've been calling them a prospect when they really are a No or a Not Right Now.

Remember James's motto, "My second favorite word is no"? That should be your second favorite word as well. No sales leader expects you to close 100 percent of what you put in the pipeline. In fact, you'll probably only close between 20 to 30 percent of what you put in, so be honest with yourself and the prospect about the reality of them becoming a customer. Give your prospect permission to tell you No or Not Right Now. You're not creating the No; it's already there. You're just helping them be honest with you so you can be honest with yourself. Although not happy news, trust me, you'd rather have a No or a Not Right Now than keep investing in the Maybe.

Your company may have (should have) established criteria for moving a deal to the "Lost" stage, but if they don't, then you need to establish it for yourself. Understand that a deal closing as Lost isn't a bad thing. It's being honest and acknowledging this prospect:

- Was misqualified and isn't a good fit.
- Doesn't have the financial resources currently.
- Wasn't high enough on the food chain to get the deal approved.
- Did not see the value.
- Just wasn't ready, for whatever reason.

Closing a deal as Lost is painful but prudent. You need to have a clear picture of what you're really working with to hit your sales goals. Kidding yourself and your sales leader is a good way to get yourself and your sales leader fired or, at the very least, make you look less like a professional sales rep and more like an amateur gambler. Because that's what you're doing, gambling with your quota, commission, and career.

The good news is that not all Nos are lost forever. If you're fortunate enough to actually get a no over the phone, in person, or in an email reply, be grateful. Remember, your goal is always to move 'em on or move 'em out. But even though you're grateful to not be wasting your time if they're not interested, I recommend you make every effort to understand the *why* behind their No or their failure to move forward to help you determine if they should be moved out of your sales cycle and into your nurturing process.

If they really don't fit your ICP or there is another compelling reason they will never buy, then wish them the best and move 'em out. But if the No is being driven by budget issues, bad timing, not enough pain currently to justify spending money, or some other circumstance, and they do fit your ICP but the timing isn't right, then think of them as a Not Right Now (NRN) instead of a No.

The NRNs need to be handled differently than Nos that purchased another product, told you to get lost, or just didn't fit your ICP. NRNs need to be nurtured and treated as future buyers instead of thrown away like last year's fruit cake. NRNs most likely just aren't ready to enter into the buyer's journey, but when they are ready, you want to make sure you are their first call.

With a good nurturing process in place, your No pile can be a "Set it and forget it" operation so you can put all your attention into your Yes pile without closing the door on the Nos. Remember when you had to touch every piece of paper in the stack to work the pipeline and you were missing opportunities because you weren't able to focus on the actual prospects likely to say yes? Well, those days are gone. You now touch only the pages in your Yes pile when you work your pipeline, so you can put all your time into moving those pages through the sales process. And you can be brutally honest about who should be in your No pile, remembering you aren't closing the door on them, you're just not putting time into trying to push them through it if they aren't ready to go.

Homework for Setting Up Your Negotiation and Nurturing Process:

- Decide how you'll nurture your NRNs and your Closed/Lost prospects.
- Go through your current pipeline and move to Close/Lost any deal that isn't active and you know is stalled.
- Invest some time and money into some professional development around negotiation and then create a negotiation framework for yourself.
- Determine when you'll be willing to negotiate.
- Create a list of "gives" you'll be willing to negotiate on and what "gets" you'll want in return.

17

Your Unique Value Proposition

I f there is anything that all rock stars have in common, it's their understanding of what makes them unique and their ability to leverage it in their chosen genre. They don't conform for the sake of conforming; they break the rules, if necessary, to be the rock stars they were meant to be. They know what works for them, and they aren't going to get trapped into doing what works for someone else. The same goes for Rock Star sales reps.

Now, that isn't a free pass to give the middle finger to your sales manager or demand green M&Ms in the conference room. That's a challenge for you to create a strategy and process for turning your personal superpowers, swim lane advantage, and secret weapons into an unbeatable and inimitable combination.

I suppose you could call this your "personal brand," but I prefer to call it your personal unique value proposition (UVP). Because it's not based on a one-dimensional persona that you develop based on who you want people to think you are; it's based on the qualities that are authentically you, that you've identified, honed, practiced, and perfected.

Your brand, or UVP, is how you're remembered by anyone who comes into contact with you. It's the reputation that lets people know what they can expect from you every time they come into contact with you. An authentically presented UVP gives you a head start on any relationship with a referred prospect, an introduction to a new mentor, colleague, or referral partner, or your next employer.

Another advantage of having already decided how you're going to show up as a sales professional is that you can use your UVP as a determining factor when you're looking for an ideal fit in a company, product, or role. If your unique value proposition is based on your authentic personality traits and designed to highlight your superpowers, you'll want to choose opportunities that allow you to be that person, no holds barred, without conflict with the company culture or brand.

So take stock: how do you show up when you're at your best and most authentic? For example, I might be (and have been) best described as super-direct, irreverent, fun-loving and funny, smart, and not for everyone—but someone who is dead serious about getting sh*t done and making things happen. That means I'm not everyone's cup of tea, but when I'm a fit, I'm such a perfect fit that I blow away the competition.

Now it's your turn. We often find it difficult to describe ourselves honestly and accurately, so you may want to enlist people who know you to be mirrors so you can see yourself through their eyes. You can do that by asking them one simple question: "How would you describe me when I'm at my absolute best?" Ask longtime friends, previous coworkers and employers, teachers and coaches, recent friends, and acquaintances. You can ask your whole social network if you want to but don't put too much stock in those answers.

If you get stuck, or if you just love metaphors and games, you might have fun asking questions like, "If I were a car, what kind of car would I be?" Or, playing along with our rock star theme, "If I were a famous musician, who would I be?" Then use that to distill some characteristics, like a Volvo is dependable and solid, a Ferrari is fast, luxurious, and expensive.

Or Prince was a reclusive introvert, and Beyonce is a gregarious entertainer and storyteller.

Remember that choosing your top traits doesn't mean that's all you are. Just because you've decided to focus on your authentic tendency to show up as outspoken or boisterous doesn't mean you can't also be dependable. The aim is to highlight what comes most naturally, what you love about yourself, and what other people can rely on you for.

Now, remember that list of Rock Star traits you created in Section One? Add them to this list of personal characteristics and start distilling it until you can list five or six descriptors of who you are when you're at your best.

Feels pretty good, doesn't it? It should. But it isn't your UVP. Not yet. Your unique value proposition isn't just who you are or how you're going to show up; it's the *value* of who you are and how you show up. This is where the real differentiation happens.

From my days of waiting tables or negotiating with Marty at Mudd, I've been known for my direct and irreverent style. But as I matured, I had to decide how I was going to turn that natural style into something uniquely valuable. I learned the difference between irreverent and downright abrasive the hard way over the years. There was one particularly tough conversation Dean had with me a few years after we'd been working together that went something like this, "It's not what you say, but how you say it." I could have gone on the defensive and insisted I was just being "authentic," but it was obvious to me that being direct and irreverent added value, and being abrasive subtracted value. I made the decision to enlist the help of a coach to double down on my authentic personality in a way that added value.

To create your UVP, take your list of top descriptors and list all the reasons they make you valuable. For instance, being known for being direct helps me build trust quickly. Being known for being fun-loving and funny not only helps me build trust, but it also helps me be approachable in the often intimidating role of consultant and coach. Being known for being smart means people come to me to solve problems, and being known for being dead serious about getting sh*t done and making things happen means people are willing to pay my fees because they know I'm going to get results.

I could go much deeper into how I built my own UVP, but this isn't about me; it's about you. It's about you deciding what you want to be known for and how each of the authentic traits you choose to highlight make you more valuable.

This decision may be the most important one we've covered in this section. More important than deciding on stages in your leads funnel, more important than deciding on your networking strategy. Deciding which traits to highlight and designing a process for intentionally doubling down on the authentic traits that bring the most value to your prospects, customers, coworkers, colleagues, and communities will pay dividends for the rest of your career, if not the rest of your life.

Homework for Defining Your Unique Value Proposition:

- Go back to Section One and make a list of the Rock Star traits you listed there.
- Make a list of the people who you trust to reflect your personality traits back to you. Include people from your childhood through your present, as well as people who know you professionally and people who only know you personally.
- Ask them this question, "How would you describe me when I'm at my absolute best?"
- Add their answers to the list of Rock Star traits.
- Look for themes and similarities, consolidate, and distill the descriptors until you have five or six that you're going to choose to be known for.
- Write out all the ways that each of those traits creates value for others.
- Decide on your process for practicing those traits, really showing up as the person who owns those traits.
- Consider hiring a coach to help you refine the way you show up.

If you have made it this far and done the homework I've given you, you're already better prepared to become the Rock Star sales rep you want to become than many seasoned reps. Now it's time to take everything you've learned about yourself and about your process and put it into action.

SECTION THREE

Bringing It All Together and Creating Abundance

At this point, if you've been doing the work I've given you, you've taken a mental inventory of what your life is currently like, you know you can have a different life, a better life, a more fulfilling life, and you've made the decision to use a career in sales to sell your way into the life you really want. A life filled with financial freedom, choices, and pride in knowing you've become a Top 10 Percenter.

Candidates often ask me during the interview what it will take to be successful in sales. With a bit of sass but just as much seriousness, I say it takes a three-year commitment to the same company or at least in the same market and industry.

My experience tells me that any sales role you choose gets exponentially easier at the three-year mark. Depending on what you're selling, how long your sales cycle is, and what your average sale is, it could take up to a year to really understand your industry and product and build your pipeline up to the level needed to consistently hit quota. That means in year two, you're starting to get into a rhythm of prospecting, maintaining your pipeline at the level needed to reach your goal, and closing deals.

By year three, you've found and committed to a process and strategy that works for you, you've started to establish yourself as an industry expert and trusted advisor, you're getting referrals from happy clients and networking relationships, and you find that some of those Not Right Nows you've been nurturing over the past two years have decided *now* is the right time, and you're starting to get those golden emails with the subject line, "Let's talk."

If you've been following your process consistently, you should have "earned the right" to have the phone ring, and you can focus on having an even higher return on every "right move" and conversation. But to do that, you'll do more than just commit to one company or one market and industry. You'll commit to yourself and to your vision of the life you're selling your way into.

I often tell my son, when he apologizes for not following through on something I've asked him to do, "If you just did it right the first time, you'd never have to apologize." This is why it's so important to do the work in the first section as early in your career as possible—because not doing something the right way the first time around (or for the first three years) is a waste of time.

It actually takes the same amount of time and mental energy to hit that Top 10 Percent and become a real sales Rock Star as it does to be an underperformer or an average performer. Underperformers spend their time and mental energy worrying about missing quota, their job security, and whether they'll have enough money to pay rent instead of using that same time and energy bettering themselves and committing to their craft. Average performers hit quota and coast. Rock Stars exceed quota, set their own bar, and do what they need to do in those three years to make raising the bar easier every year after that. This is what we call selling your way *in*.

After you've spent those three years committed to doing your work, personally and professionally, you're ready for the payoff. You've invested in yourself and your career by understanding who you are, what your sales strengths and superpowers are, and what type of sales job you are the most successful at, and you've put the time in practicing your skills to perfection. All of the decisions you've made, job roles you've chosen, and coaches and mentors you've added to your team are having a cumulative effect, just like compound interest. Now you've earned the right to have the life you want.

Becky is one shining example of the three-year rule. It's been my pleasure over the past fifteen years to watch this former employee sell her way into an amazing life for herself and her family. I hired Becky in my sixth year as VP of Sales at the elearning company, and almost immediately, I knew she was cut from a different cloth. One of the main reasons I hired Becky was because her prior company had given her strong, foundational, professional sales training. As I suspected, she onboarded quickly and had a strong desire to learn everything about the product, the industry, and the sales process in as short a time as possible.

It wasn't just that Becky was well-trained and smarter than most that set her apart; she also had as strong a work ethic as I'd seen. She wasn't there to socialize or make friends. There's nothing wrong with having work buddies, but that wasn't her purpose or focus. She was there to sell and to make money. Period. She wasn't driven by recognition, promotions, or titles. She knew all that would be a byproduct of her ability to outsell everyone else in the office and the top competitors in her field as well. She and I spent many hours, after everyone else had gone home, talking shop and strategizing to ensure she hit her personal revenue goals, which often exceeded the ones the company had set for her. At some point, I became less a boss and more of a mentor.

Our relationship continued even after I left that company, four years after Becky came onboard. Her drive to outearn everyone around her continued for six more years. During that time, she earned what I refer to as "A-player privilege." She requested and was approved to work from home permanently after giving birth to her first child. When I asked her about her desire to leave the office and work from home, she said there were two reasons: First, eliminating her commute and hiring a nanny allowed her more time with her child before and after work. Second, she didn't feel like there was anyone at her level in the company, and with no one there to mentor the junior reps, they were constantly coming to her for help and advice, which was not what she was hired to do and was a distraction she didn't want as she was trying to reach a new level of success. Like all Top 10 Percenters, Becky knew she needed to say no more than she said yes.

Ten years after I hired Becky at the elearning company, they put a new policy in place that rubbed up against her value system. She reached out to me for advice. Over lunch at our favorite sushi restaurant, I listened as she told me about the new policy and how it made her feel. I shared with her a similar experience I had while in retail that created a conflict with my value system. While I hated to see her walk away from the amazing career she'd built over the past ten years at that company, I knew that making a change now wouldn't put the life she'd built at risk.

Becky left the privately-owned elearning company and joined a venture capital-backed, elearning startup out of Silicon Valley. She consulted with me during the interview process, and I was happy she had made the decision to stay in elearning. I knew staying in the same industry would help her get up and running more quickly, making it more likely that she'd stay at her current earning level.

One thing I hadn't factored in when advising Becky on her next move was whether or not she would be a good fit at a startup. Unfortunately, the product was half-baked, and the sales strategy and product market fit were still in beta. I was already fully entrenched in the startup world at that point and couldn't have been happier, but a good startup-fit employee needs to be more willow than oak, (meaning flexible, not ridged) and Becky, well, she was an oak tree. She wanted a product that was competitive in the market, a formal and tested sales process, and great onboarding to help her get off to a fast start. None of these things were in place.

Not surprisingly, my phone rang about three months after she started, resulting in another lunch meeting over sushi. She shared what she'd figured out about the stage the company was really in versus the impression she'd gotten while interviewing. I encouraged her to give it a few more months to see if, with more time in the oven, what looked undercooked might end up as a gourmet dish.

Three months later, Becky reached out to let me know that the oven temperature never seemed to get above 250 degrees and she was starting to look for a new job. Her situation sounded eerily similar to a situation I had gotten myself into a few years ago that turned out to be nothing like I thought, and I knew it was time for Becky to make a move. I asked her how I could support her, and she asked if I would be a reference for her as she began to interview. I not only agreed to do that, but I also set out to see if I could help her find her next home.

Sixty days later, Becky called to let me know she was interviewing with a more mature elearning company, albeit a VC-backed company, and she'd put me down as a reference. I was enjoying a little fresh air on my deck when I got the reference call from the VP of Sales at the company Becky was interviewing with. He and I hit it off immediately, bonding over our love of all things sales, elearning, and startups. Like all good reference checks, he asked me what he might struggle with managing Becky. I laughed and said, "She's a bit of a lone wolf. Don't expect her to form friendships, volunteer to help train the new hires, or sign up to chair the holiday committee. If you want Becky to perform at her peak, show her the formula, get out of her way, and support her when she comes for help. If that aligns with your culture and your values as a sales leader, then she's the woman for the job." She got the job, and twelve months later, she posted a picture from Hawaii. She'd made President's Club in her first year.

I'm so proud of Becky. She was strong enough to leave a job that didn't align with her value system, she was self-aware enough to leave the next position in under twelve months when she figured out it wasn't the right step-change for her, and then she made the right step-change by taking a job with a more mature elearning company— in the first year making President's Club. Becky knows the elearning space as well as any rep in the industry. She has a tried-and-true process that she's perfected over the past fifteen years, and her work ethic is as strong as ever. All of these success factors combined have allowed her to build the life we used to talk about during those after-hours conversations over ten years ago.

The moral of this story is that Becky spent the first three years with the elearning company doing exactly what this book is challenging you and teaching you to do. She not only committed to the company, the industry, and the market, but she also committed to herself and her vision. She knew her strengths, her swim lane, and her secret weapon. And she played to those strengths while keeping her eye on what she really wanted.

Whether you're upleveling in your role at the same company, changing roles, or changing companies, you now have the formula to be a "Becky" and sell your way into any lifestyle you choose, just as Becky did.

You may be thinking to yourself that you might not enjoy working with Becky. She doesn't seem "teamy," and you'd be right—she's not. That "attitude," if you will, worked for her for two reasons. One, because she knew her strengths, swim lane, and secret weapons, and she knew she wasn't a teacher, trainer, or mentor by nature. She knew trying to be Miss Helpful wasn't the best use of her talent or energy. Becky was pure hunter and a natural lone-wolf hunter at that. Recognizing that strength and playing to it was not only what made her successful in achieving what she wanted in her career, it was hugely successful for the companies she worked for if they let her play to those strengths.

When I say, "Be a Becky," I'm not suggesting that you adopt her lone-wolf style. Not all hunters need to be a lone wolf to succeed. In fact, most of them enjoy interaction and belonging to a team; they just won't focus on nurturing. And, as we've discussed, not every successful sales rep is a hunter. The point I'm making is for you to spend those first three years on *your* strengths, swim lane, and secret weapons, and you'll find your true fit and earn Rock Star status the way Becky did.

The second reason that Becky's lone-wolf selling style worked for her was because it worked for me, her sales leader. Not every sales leader wants a lone wolf on their team, so I warn leaders that a true hunter will lean more lone wolf than team player. I tell them, "Be careful what you ask for; you just might get it," as was the case with Melanie.

I began working with Melanie as her executive coach during the pandemic after she heard me on Jeb Blount's *Sales Gravy Podcast*. She was a new sales leader and wanted someone who could support and coach her during her first few months in her new role.

During one coaching session, she was complaining that her team wasn't being teamy. "What do you mean?" I asked. She said she'd asked each rep to do a mini-training session on something they felt they were particularly good at and share their strategy with the team during the weekly sales meeting, but a few of the reps weren't following through and showing up unprepared. "I want them to be a team and help each other out," she said. I immediately thought of Becky.

So I shared the good and bad news with her. The good news was the ones who weren't showing up prepared were probably true hunters. The ones who came with thirty-five slides in a deck and walk-on music probably weren't. She just stared at me over Zoom with a confused look on her face. "What do you mean?" she asked. I told her true Top 10 Percenters are focused on reaching that Top 10 Percent, and that can look like being selfish. For hunters, that means not giving their time and energy to anything but selling. They have goals they want to accomplish, and they're going to see coaching other reps as taking time away from achieving their mission. Her eyes got big, and then she said she'd been mis-hiring. She'd been looking for team players, not hunters.

Make it your responsibility to find your true fit in terms of culture and leadership. If you know you're a hunter, make sure you're in a role that supports you. If you know you're a farmer, make sure you're in a role where you can hit your success goals while nurturing and growing client relationships. Play to your strengths in those three years, and you'll become exponentially stronger. Same with learning every nuance of your swim lane or honing your secret weapon. Spend the first three years drilling those skills, and every year after that will yield a return on that investment.

In this section, we're going to go beyond those first three years and get into some master strategies for keeping your Rock Star status for as long as you choose to be in sales.

18

Mastering the Mental

As I've grown myself and my business, I've realized there is one thing more than any other that I wish I'd known much earlier in my life and that I wish I could instill in every single person I know. It's this: you really are in complete control of your life and your future, and the difference between the life you have and the life you want is all in your head—literally.

Here are a few more things that fall under the category of "What I wish my younger self had known":

1. Self-talk is as important as physical practice.
2. Visualization can change the future.
3. Bad and unpleasant things will happen, but there is always something to be grateful for.
4. The only limits are the ones you place on yourself.
5. Your circle matters.
6. Judge less and listen more.
7. Daily affirmations spoken out loud will imprint on your mind.

I remember the first time I truly understood the power of my mind. I was in my late teens and was taking a private lesson with my racquetball coach, Pete. We were working on a forehand drill, using one of the cans the balls came in as a target. I took some practice swings to get the muscle memory to kick in and started the drill. I hit the can a few times but not as often as Pete thought I should, and I made some smart-a$$ comment about it being hard or not being able to master it. I groused that, of course, it was easier for him; he'd been playing racquetball for something like seventeen years (which was about how long I'd been alive, so it was like forever!), and he couldn't expect me to be that good yet.

You remember the story of how Mike Weinberg, many years later, taught me a lesson in acknowledging the strengths I'd already mastered when he coached me into starting my business and setting my fees to match my abilities? Well, Pete didn't buy into my self-doubts any more than Mike did. He decided to demonstrate how my body already knew how to hit the target; I was just letting my mind tell me that it was "hard" and that because I hadn't been doing it as long as Pete had, I couldn't be as good as Pete said I was.

He told me to grab a bandana off my racquetball bag and come back onto the court. As I reentered, I saw that he'd taken the two blue racquetballs out of their can and was setting up the empty can against the front wall. "OK," he said, "take a good look at where the can is." After giving him side-eye, I did as I was told. He then instructed me to put on the blindfold. Hmmm. This was getting weird. "Now," he said, "hit the can."

"What?" I lifted the blindfold from over one eye and came back at him with my trademark sass.

Pete didn't blink. "You said you saw it. Now visualize it again in your mind exactly where you saw it and drill it with your forehand."

Now, how in the world am I supposed to make contact with the ball I'm holding in my hand, let alone hit a target I can't even see? I thought.

"Go ahead," Pete prodded.

So I took another good look at the can against the wall, lowered the blindfold, and tossed the ball up as I would without the blindfold and hit it. I heard the ball hit the front wall.

"Close," Pete informed me as he went and chased down the ball I'd hit and returned it to me.

"Try again."

I visualized where I had seen the can and then replicated the motion and almost instantaneously, I heard the can explode. I ripped off the blindfold to see the can with a massive dent and the blue rubber lid lying close to it. The grin on my face was almost as big as the one on Pete's face. *Wow! That was super empowering!*

"If you can hit the target blindfolded, then you shouldn't have any issue hitting it with both eyes open!" Pete exclaimed. He was right. It was all about keeping my eye on the ball but also about visualizing that ball going exactly where I wanted it to go.

From that day forward, I not only visualized shaking hands as the winner after a tennis match but also enjoying a lazy day on a private beach with the man I love. I still fully embrace the power of my mind and all the amazing things I can manifest if I choose.

The key word here is *choose*. You can choose to be frustrated and pissy when things aren't going your way, or you can dig in and use all the available tools you have at your disposal to manifest a more fulfilling future for you and your family. And by all available tools, I mean a whole range of mental training tools, not only visualization but also gratitude, speaking affirmations out loud, and positive self-talk.

Visualization is powerful, as I learned on the racquetball court, but it shouldn't be confused with daydreaming. Daydreaming has no direction or purpose and is mostly unconscious. Visualization is a conscious thought process with a very specific desired outcome. You see the end results you want, and you imprint that outcome in your mind so your mind will work to ensure that what you visualized will come to life.

I feel just as strongly about positive self-talk and speaking affirmations out loud. When I'm out on the tennis court and things aren't going my way or my energy level is low, I repeat these two phrases: "You're the winner" and "Win this point." I want my brain to kick my body into gear and get on the winning program. I don't always win every match, but I couldn't look my teammates in the eye when I came off the court if I didn't use every tool available, and that includes my mental tools.

Tennis is just my hobby and happy place, but it's a good case study for what happens when I apply the same concepts to my life and career goals. Winning is the same mental game in life, business, and tennis!

Positive self-talk is another powerful tool. It's so easy to get down on yourself and engage in negative self-talk. A few years ago, my son started to say, "I'm so stupid" when he'd do something, well, stupid. I didn't think much about it until I heard Brené Brown's "Power of Vulnerability" seminar, and she said you need to stop saying "you are" and start saying "you did."

So I explained to my son that he might have done something stupid, but that didn't make him stupid and he needed to change his self-talk to "That was stupid," or better yet, "I guess I wasn't thinking."

This one is harder. You need to be as compassionate and supportive with yourself as you would be with a friend who was taking a big risk or struggling with something. You wouldn't jump on the bandwagon and tell your friend she wasn't smart enough to be promoted or ask her when she thought she might be asked to pack her box. You'd reassure her that she is just as smart and capable as the other candidates and coworkers or that this, too, shall pass and best to chalk it up to a lesson learned.

How we talk to ourselves is really a way of telling ourselves what we believe about ourselves. If our talk is all blame and doubt, the belief we're communicating is that we are a person who does things wrong and will probably keep on doing things wrong. If our talk is full of compassion and commitment, we're communicating the belief that we make mistakes, and by recognizing the mistake and #owningourownshit, we can *and will* do better in the future.

I've also added verbal affirmations to my daily routine. I start every day saying, "Today is the best day for/to _____. I usually fill that blank with something like personal growth, a new relationship, financial success, learning something new, or similar aspirations. I usually add a little more color commentary in, but I want to make sure I set my intentions for each day.

What if every day, before you fired up the computer, you said out loud, "Today is the best day to successfully prospect," or "Today is the best day to close the deal I've been working on?" What if you were brave enough to take it one step further and said to yourself, "I am good enough," or "I deserve happiness and success?"

And what if you told yourself this every day? How long do you think it would take before you not only believed it, but before it imprinted on your mind? Powerful.

I started using out-loud verbal affirmations after I added a hypnotherapist to my "team." She was in a mastermind group I belonged to called Kick Ass Chicks. (Hint: having a mastermind group you engage with regularly is another tool in the arsenal.) This group is made up of women entrepreneurs who meet monthly to share ideas, solve problems, and support each other. I'd been in the group with Michelle for a couple of years when it occurred to me that her services might be an interesting addition to my mental game.

I know you might be thinking I'm blessed to have the financial resources to add Michelle to the team and see her quarterly, and you're right. But ask yourself whether I can afford Michelle because I'm successful or if I am successful because of Michelle and the other coaches and mentors I've added to my team. This is just part of my commitment to use every tool I can to create the life I want to live.

We met in her office, and she asked me what made me call. I told her I had some lofty goals that year, and I needed all the help and positivity I could get. She asked questions around what my specific goals were and what challenges I might bump up against. No surprise if you've been paying attention, but I asked her to specifically address my fear around raising my rates and charging more. In general, I wanted her to fill my unconscious with words around how strong, smart, and successful I am and how I effortlessly solve challenges that are presented to me when they arise.

Michelle says I'm hypno-friendly. I think this is because I believe the mind is the "twelfth man." This is a phase used in football. There are eleven players for each team on the field for every play. The twelfth man is the hometown crowd supporting and cheering on their team from the stands. Interestingly, the twelfth man usually comes into play when the home team is behind, and the players rally the support of the fans to help them turn their current situation around.

A mind that is trained to be the twelfth man can be the difference between the life you have now and the life you could have. Use your mind as your twelfth man to encourage and support you when you're getting ready to make that do-or-die presentation to your client's executive team or when you're struggling to get that enterprise deal across the finish line. I hope you have people you can count on to cheer you on, but one of my Kristieisms is that sometimes you must "bring your own pom poms" and be your own cheerleader.

Speaking of your circle, as I've discussed throughout the book, your circle matters. They say everyone comes into your life for a reason, a season, or a lifetime. I've found this to be true. That means not everyone who comes into your life was meant to stay. Be selective about who you bring into your circle, personally and professionally, while also being aware when a relationship might have served its purpose and can add little or no value moving forward.

As I've continued to grow personally and professionally and challenge myself to be better each day, I've had to accept that there are those who aren't going to be interested or capable of coming on the journey with me. For me, I know that if I want to grow as a person and take my career as far as I can, I'll need to be leveling up my team and my circle every step of the way.

There's one last way you need to stretch your mind to ensure you can have the life you want. You need to understand the concept of abundance. The definition of abundance according to Cambridge Dictionary is, "The situation in which there is more than enough of something." To have abundance, you need an abundance mindset.

You can live in a world of abundance, or you can live in a world of limitations, either/or, or what if. The choice is yours. Accepting that there is plenty all around you will help you see opportunities you've never seen before and understand that it's not either work or family—that you can have both. Asking "What if X doesn't work out?" isn't getting you where you want to go. Limitations are fear-based. You must push that fear aside to open up the possibilities that await you.

Living in a world of abundance is to believe you can have it all, and I'm not just speaking of financial wealth. You can have an abundance of love for others, an abundance of time, and an abundance of friendships. Using visualization or affirmations will help you create abundance in your life. Visualize the life you want so when it starts to manifest, you'll recognize it. What your mind sees, it will strive to bring to life. Use positive affirmations to open the mind to new possibilities and help you reduce your negative and limiting thoughts.

Over time, you'll see opportunities and possibilities everywhere instead of roadblocks and danger signs. There really is enough of everything in the world for everyone to have what they desire. The possibilities for you are endless. You just need to decide what you want and speak it into the Universe, and when you start to produce more than you need for yourself, you can begin to bless others who are still on their way to abundance.

The thing to remember is visualization and mindset build a foundation, but abundance comes from taking action on the vision. I regularly get calls from people who say, "I want to be you when I grow up." They love what I've built for myself, and they want to know how to have it for themselves. I tell them, "Come on in; the water's warm, and there are plenty of clients for all of us." But very few actually put on their swimsuits and jump in the pool.

19

Leveraging What You've Created

The best time to push harder is when things are going well and success is happening. As the book *Good to Great* by James C. Collins advocates, it's much easier to take something you're good at, put in a little more effort, and turn it into something you're great at, as I did with my slice forehand. Now that you're starting to see how the work you've been putting in is allowing you to manifest the life you want, it's time to step on the accelerator, not coast or put on the brakes.

There are three things you can focus on to help you build on your current success:

1. Strengthen relationships; turn casual acquaintances into enthusiastic colleagues and good friends into loyal advocates.
2. Sow to grow; invest in yourself and your success.
3. Nurture your garden; take good care of the seeds you've planted along the way.

Strengthen Relationships

The right relationships can be the difference between getting to 100 percent versus being stuck at 90 percent. Think about how to really leverage the relationships you've been building personally and professionally. Who in your circle could you connect with on a deeper and more meaningful level? Who could be a mentor? Who could you swap leads with so you both win? Where could you add value to your circle?

This goes to my "I have thirty minutes for everyone" mantra. I say this often to all kinds of people and lo and behold, people take me up on it--sometimes for themselves but most often they reach out to see if I'd be willing to help someone in their circle. It's something I enjoy doing—helping others—and it endears me to the person I helped as well as the person who connected them with me. So I'm getting a twofer out of it. Every time I provide thirty minutes of free consulting and support, I'm strengthening a relationship and putting good juju into the Universe.

Going the extra mile and adding some special touches will ensure these people will be "working" for you while you might have your attention elsewhere. Give thought to what might be of value to them and start to put those thoughts into action. A new customer you just sold to would surely appreciate a handwritten thank you note from you but would appreciate an introduction from you to a possible prospect even more. This falls under "The Platinum Rule" or "Treat others the way they want to be treated, not the way you would want to be treated." Try to get to know people in your circle well enough to craft custom ways to show you care, are thinking of them, or want to help them succeed.

I had a guy in my circle a few years ago whom I didn't know very well—until one day I had an opportunity to attend a breakout session he led at a tech startup event. I learned during his session that instead of cold prospecting, he found prospects by helping them connect with people who might be a good prospect for them. He shared with the group that he had a goal of networking with five new people a week who were all connected to other people he knew. *WOW!* I thought. *How in the world does he have time to do that?* The answer: he made time because it was the personal process he decided would work best for him.

He was right. I already had my "Thirty minutes for everyone" motto, but I wasn't proactively reaching out to people to offer my time. I went up to him after his session and said I thought we should meet for coffee. That was four years ago, and today, we're in a mastermind group together, and he's one of the first people I think of when I say, "I wonder who would know . . ."

Sow to Grow

The second area you can always be working on is what I call #sowtogrow. That Kristieism was partly inspired by this quote:

> *"Sow a thought, and you reap an act; Sow an act, and you reap a habit; Sow a habit and you reap a character; Sow a character, and you reap a destiny."* —Stephen Covey

When you hear the word *sow*, I bet your mind goes to "You reap what you sow," which is biblically associated with negative consequences. But what if you flipped the script and decided to sow seeds that produce a fruitful harvest for years to come? Planting those seeds consistently will ensure new plants of abundance are always breaking through the soil.

In other words, you must: #ownyourstrengths, #ownyourownshit, and #sowtogrow before you can play to your strengths or leverage them to become a Top 10 Percenter.

Personal development or personal growth is often seen as a way to "work on yourself" or "overcome your weaknesses." But honestly, the most successful sales careers are built by people who understand they need to continuously invest in personal development to fully own and leverage the strengths they already have. They record and listen to their calls. They seek feedback from other Rock Stars. They invest time in reading blog posts, attending training webinars, listening to podcasts, and following sales thought leaders online. You must be intentional about how you sow your seeds for growth as it relates to your strengths to have a robust harvest.

If any of my mentors have completely modeled the sow-to-grow mindset for me, it has to be my Uncle Bill. He is my father's brother and was the original owner of the real estate business my father took over when we moved to Topeka. The original plan when my father joined the agency was that Uncle Bill would move to Arizona to retire. But the entrepreneur in him wasn't ready to be idle, and he continued to sell and invest in real estate. He parlayed his first self-storage facility into a second, then bought an apartment complex that no one else would invest in, and brokered a win-win deal with a nearby addiction and mental health treatment center to convert those apartments into exclusive furnished living spaces for the patients' families to stay in when they came in for visits and family counseling.

Uncle Bill, or Pecos, as the family calls him, is hugely successful by anyone's standards. But his success isn't due to his savvy real estate investments. It's because he's always invested in himself, in other people, and in doing the right thing at the right time, and then letting the right things come back to him.

Pecos embodies a principle he calls "selling by trust." Selling by trust requires trusting himself first and always investing in building trust with others, putting that trust before any deal or financial gain. That means he has to be ready and willing to walk away from a client or steer a client away from a deal if it isn't the best solution because to do anything else would violate that trust. Because of his unwavering belief in unlimited abundance and opportunity, he is almost always able to do both.

As he says, he isn't really selling in the sense that most people think of selling. He's always known the thing he was really selling was himself, so he worked on building a high level of trust with his prospects. And if a prospect showed they weren't willing to trust him or they kept him at arm's length, he knew that wasn't someone he wanted to work with. Because he recognized what he was sowing would be what was growing later, he consistently said, "No, thanks" to those people, no matter what kind of deal he might have eventually been able to close.

Uncle Bill didn't start sowing to grow *after* he'd made his money in real estate. He had that mindset from the beginning, and it's one of the reasons he's been so successful in real estate and everything else. He told me a story from his early days in sales that not only highlights the importance of the #sowtogrow mindset but is also a textbook lesson in #dotherightthings.

He hadn't been in real estate very long when a man came to see him about looking at a home for his family. Uncle Bill took the time to chat so they could get to know each other and so he could really understand what this man wanted in a home. Among other things, he told Uncle Bill it was really important to him to be in a good neighborhood. He had several children and needed a larger home, but he was concerned that his finances wouldn't allow him to qualify for a larger home in a neighborhood that would offer his children the safety and opportunities he wanted them to have.

They made a list of homes to tour, and one of them was an older home the buyer really loved. In fact, he was quite vocal with Uncle Bill about how perfect it was. It could have been a "slam dunk," which is a great feeling when you're just starting out in real estate. But there was one problem.

As they walked back to his car, Uncle Bill said, "I know you love this home, but I don't believe this is all that great of a neighborhood."

The buyer obviously loved the house, and it could have been at the top of his list. He also knew it would have been easy for Uncle Bill to sell him that home and hope the kids would be okay. But because Uncle Bill lived in abundance and put trust-building above wealth-building, he knew there were more than enough houses to show this buyer, more than enough prospects to replace this buyer if his honesty should cause this relationship to go south, and more than enough opportunities to work with people who trusted him if this man did not. He knew he could afford to #dotherightthing because he had no fears about "What if X doesn't work out?" He knew there were at least twenty-five other letters in the alphabet, and X really didn't matter enough to compromise his values over it.

Of course, he didn't lose that buyer. When he shared his concerns about the neighborhood, the buyer looked him square in the eyes and said, "I appreciate that statement so much. Just take me and show me whatever you think is best."

"The buyer," in Uncle Bill's words, "now trusted me like a brother and was interested in whatever recommendations I had." By staying true to his principle of selling by trust, he not only created that sale, but he also created a relationship, a reputation, and a highly successful real estate business. What he was sowing in his early years has grown into a life of abundance and fulfillment.

Prospecting is where the combination of #ownyourstrengths, #ownyourownshit, and #sowtogrow create exponential success and the ability to #ownyourincome. As we discussed earlier in the book, I work hard to convince sales reps that consistent prospecting will lead to a consistent pipeline, and a consistently full pipeline will lead to you consistently hitting your quota.

I know if you fail to prospect, you might as well plan to fail. But how you create your strategy and process for keeping the pipeline filled is up to you. It takes being accountable and disciplined, combined with consistently investing in your pipeline, to keep you off the feast or famine roller coaster. That roller coaster ride starts when your pipeline is full and you stop prospecting, then lo and behold, you've closed out half your pipeline (won and lost), and now you must throw everything you've got into outbound prospecting.

A few years back, I "inherited" a rep named Ashley when I joined a SaaS company as VP of Sales and Customer Success. I didn't find Ashley particularly warm or outgoing, but her numbers indicated she knew what she was doing and that she was a top performer. As I met one-on-one with all my new sales reps, Ashley stood out. She shared that she was a very structured and organized person. I asked more about how she structured her day, and she replied, "I block my calendar from 9:00 a.m. to noon every day, and that's when I prospect. I do all of my demos, follow-up calls, and other meetings in the afternoons."

"Wow!" I said. "That's very disciplined."

She agreed.

I asked her what happened if a prospect who was already in the pipeline wanted to meet in the morning. She replied that she did her best to find an afternoon time that worked for both of them. Why? Because she knew mornings were her most successful time to prospect, and she wasn't going to spend them doing anything else. But she also had discipline around how she invested in demos and follow-up calls; she was doing her #sowtogrow activities just as consistently as she was her prospecting.

I never saw Ashley on the feast or famine prospecting roller coaster. That was eight years ago, and I have yet to find anyone who not only understands the importance of consistent prospecting but is also as committed to the mission.

One of the ways I'm personally working the #sowtogrow strategy is by being a lifelong learner. I read, listen to podcasts, surround myself with people smarter than me, and push myself to try new things. That's what helps me be ready for any unexpected opportunity that comes my way, even if it is out of my "comfort zone."

I got one of those opportunities to learn a new skill and challenge myself all at the same time just as the pandemic was beginning. A representative from Udemy for Business, an online learning platform, reached out to me on LinkedIn and said they were building out a catalog filled with sales training courses and would I be interested in talking to them about creating a course. "Sure," I said, "I've got thirty minutes!"

We got on the phone, and she explained that the business side of Udemy was starting to build out sales courses their members could take, and she thought there might be some topics I was qualified to teach. I put together an outline for two courses I thought might be valuable and presented those to the instructor selection committee, then waited to hear back. A week or so later, I was contacted and told that my proposal for a prospecting course had been given the green light!

I was excited to write my first elearning course. Having been in the elearning industry for ten years, I had some knowledge about adult learning theory and best practices around creating an interactive course, but as it turns out, I wasn't as prepared as I thought. Thank goodness Udemy had a formal process (the best always do) they take instructors through, which included being assigned an instructional designer who held my hand and held me accountable the entire way.

I naively thought I would have the course written in three months so filming and production could take place. Like all new things, it took me about twice as long to create an outline, write each section, produce the materials to support the content, and then write out the entire script that I would read during filming. It was a long process, and I learned a ton, not the least of which was that if I didn't block the first hour of my day, my day would slip away without me having made any progress on the course.

This was definitely a labor of love as opposed to a get rich quick (or slowly) scheme; to date I've only made $1,858. But 1,301 people have taken my course, and I love the thought that I might have had an impact on a new sales rep who was just starting out. This opportunity was never about the money for me; it was about the opportunity to learn a new skill from experts in the field. I'm proud of the course and proud to say I'm a Udemy for Business instructor. The outline for the course influenced the outline of this book, so I can definitely say the Udemy seeds I planted helped me have the confidence to write a book.

Nurture the Garden

Unlike my previous example, sometimes it's not as easy or as quick a correlation from planting seeds in the spring and harvesting the crop in the fall. Sometimes, to realize the full potential of something, you need to fertilize it, water it, hope the sun comes out, and keep it free of weeds— you need to nurture the seed you've been planting. You can't just decide to learn one new skill annually and call yourself a lifelong learner. You need to have a learner's mindset and always be looking for new opportunities to stretch yourself and continue to hone the superpowers you worked so hard to develop.

If I stopped using my forehand slice for a few months, it would no longer be my tennis superpower. The muscle memory I had worked so hard to develop would slowly erode, and I would no longer be able to call on that skill to save the day when I'm down a set in a best-of-three-set match. If I want to rely on it, I will need to continue to practice it in a variety of situations so that I can use it to win the points I need to win the match.

Starting over at zero is hard and frustrating, so make sure you're doing the annual maintenance needed to ensure the tulips come up every spring. You need to think about how you're going to nurture the seeds of success you've been planting over the past few months and years so all you'll need to do is add some fertilizer and set the sprinkler to help you bring a skill back to life that you might have stopped attending to for a little bit.

20

Choosing Your Three Things—The Formula You've Been Waiting For

I f you've interviewed with me in the past or think you might in the future, here's a question I guarantee you'll hear out of my mouth: "What are the three things you do consistently that ensure you're successful regardless of the position or company you're at?"

Hint: There is no right answer. I hear everything from exercising each morning, to meditating daily, to attending church regularly. Although I usually find the answers are a window into understanding the candidate better, that's not why I ask the question. I ask the question to see if *they* know the answer and can rattle it off quickly. Understanding what makes you successful and able to play at the top of your game is critical to ensuring you'll maintain that level of peak performance throughout your career. If a sales rep has awareness of their personal success formula, I know I'll have a better chance of helping them create a sales success formula that will allow them to reach the top of their profession.

If you've done the work up to this point in the book, you already have the formula for success, whether you know it or not, because you've gotten clarity around what we've already discussed, such as:

- Who you are, why you chose a sales career
- What really motivates you
- What strengths you can count on consistently
- Whether you've picked the right sales position that will allow you to become a Top 10 Percenter
- Whether you own the swim lane you're currently in or need to switch lanes
- How you can better hone your secret weapon
- Who in your circle needs to go to make room for new people who will make you a better person and what people (mentors, coaches, role models) you need to have in your corner to advance your success

That means if you've done the work up to this point, you're ready to fine-tune your process to turn it into a recipe you can depend on to yield cumulative results.

Processes require consistency. Remember Ashley from earlier in the book? Ashley had a consistent formula for prospecting that she believed would lead to her success. And she was right; it did.

She blocked time each morning to prospect. She knew herself well enough to know that if she didn't have a formula for prospecting, it wouldn't be done consistently and she'd struggle to hit quota. So she blocked the time and wouldn't let other sales activities creep into her dedicated prospecting time.

Formulas also require discipline. What good will it do you if you've gone to the trouble to create a personalized formula for your success if you then aren't disciplined enough to execute on it daily? An article in *Entrepreneur Magazine* reported on a survey of 267 C-level executives at Fortune 500 companies, and found the majority of them woke up at 6:15 a.m. each day, got forty-five minutes of exercise in before heading to the office, and spent an average of thirty minutes a day on personal development. It should come as no surprise that the most successful business leaders in our country have a consistent and disciplined routine they execute on a daily basis.

Discipline is hard. If that weren't true, we'd be a nation full of healthy-eating, exercise-loving people with enough money in the bank to retire at fifty. But that's not the case. Sixty-five percent of Americans are overweight, and only 14 percent of Americans aged fifty and up could retire tomorrow if necessary.

I like this definition of discipline: "Making yourself do something you need to do when you could be doing something more enjoyable." You need to accept that a disciplined approach to your personal and professional life will yield better results than going through each day only doing things you enjoy.

I shared in the chapter on honing your secret weapon that my forehand slice was my tennis secret weapon, and although I rely on it 90 percent of the time in matches, I also realized that only relying on my slice, forehand and backhand, would be less effective when playing good players or players whom I played against regularly. So, several years ago, I approached my coach and told him I wanted to spend the summer learning and getting comfortable with backhand topspin (hitting the ball with forward spin). So I set out, with the support of my coach, to put topspin into my game by the beginning of the next season.

I started with taking private lessons once a week to speed up the learning curve. In between lessons, my coach asked me to find a wall in my neighborhood to hit against so I could build muscle memory more quickly. This required discipline. I was working full-time, had a young child who needed my attention (i.e., parenting), and had a house to maintain, but improving my skills on the tennis court was also important to me. So I found a two-story wall at a nearby junior high school tucked away at the back of a parking lot, which I thought would be perfect for my new project. I would come home from work each night and pack up my child and his bike and head to "The Wall" to practice for thirty minutes. I brought my headset so I could play music that would motivate me and help pass the time. We did this week after week throughout the summer—that was my formula.

Little by little, I saw progress. By the end of the second month, my coach said that with only forty-five days until the start of the season, I needed to put my new skills to the test by hitting against another person instead of "The Wall." So I went about finding hitting partners who were willing to suffer through my inconsistent topspin backhand in exchange for a little cardio.

By the end of the summer, I was comfortable using my new topspin backhand in low-risk and controlled environments. But the real test would come as the season started. Did I have the guts to try it out in match play when winning and losing was on the line? As you can imagine, I had my good days using my topspin and my not-so-good days. I devised a strategy for when to force myself to put my topspin in play. I tried to use my topspin more when I was winning and then relied on my slice when the match was close or when I was down.

I'm now comfortable using my topspin when the match calls for it, and I learned a valuable lesson in the importance of having a disciplined formula when learning a new skill.

Habits Support the Formula

Once you have your formula for success fully baked, you must establish the habits that will support the formula you built. After a few weeks, going to "The Wall" after work became a habit. I no longer needed to think about or plan for it; it was just what my child and I did at the end of the day several nights a week. It was hard to be disciplined enough to go until it became a habit.

Habits help you train your brain to react automatically when a situation presents itself. "If this happens, then I automatically do this." Just as my discipline in getting myself to "The Wall" turned into an automatic routine and my practice against "The Wall" turned into the muscle memory to use my backhand topspin in competition, wiring in your success formula will lead to developing the mental memory you need to be sure you will react the same way each time a particular situation occurs. You don't want to waste any mental energy deciding what to do next in a repeatable situation. You want your next action to be automatic when faced with a situation you've encountered over and over.

There are a few universal habits among the Top 10 Percenters. One of the most powerful habits I see Top 10 Percenters using consistently is making sure they never get off a call without setting the next call, establishing the goals of the next call, and determining who will be attending.

The benefit of putting this habit in place will manifest itself in you having a way to separate the posers from the players, thereby shortening the sales cycle and experiencing a lot less frustration by not having to spend your time chasing down prospects who have already shown you their level of interest isn't that high. Most sales professionals know they *should* schedule the next firm call, Top 10 Percenters have the discipline to do it every time.

Another habit I believe separates those who succeed and those who constantly struggle is a formal post-meeting recap. This can be in the form of an email, or more recently, I've seen reps send a video recap. This recap includes what was discussed during the meeting, what homework each team has been assigned, and what the goals of the next meeting will be. Not only does this provide great documentation, but it also shows the prospect you are a true sales professional. Over the course of a three-to-six-month sales cycle, your prospect will come to expect a recap within twenty-four hours of a previous meeting.

This habit establishes that you're a person who has a plan, is consistent, and can be counted on. This consistency gives the prospect a level of comfort. It's psychological. People like predictability. Inconsistency and erratic behavior cause stress. Predictability breeds comfort. Remember, you are the face of your company. You're most likely the only person they've interacted with at your company, so the interactions you have with them will set the tone for what they will assume will be the interactions they'll have with everyone at your company.

Here's a non-sales example. I have a friend who is always on time and most times early. He thinks being late is rude and disrespectful, and he's right. But it's comforting for me to know that I will never have to sit alone at the restaurant pretending to read the menu for the fourth time because he's running late or sit alone in my car at the park, waiting to start my workout because he's caught in traffic. I know that when we make plans, I can schedule the rest of my day around that event, and I won't have to rearrange my schedule because of him. Sometimes I suggest that we meet around 6:15*ish*, just to make him a little crazy, but the truth is, I love that I can count on him to be where he says he's going to be when he says he's going to be there.

Being on time isn't something he has to think about or build a discipline around—it's just how he lives his life. The funny thing about his habit is how it's impacted me. I now make sure that I'm early when we meet. He's raised my awareness of the concept that "early is on time," and I work hard to be a couple minutes early, so it's made me a more conscientious person.

You'll find as you put more discipline and habits around your sales success formula, you'll notice those around you will raise their game too. Not just your friends, family, or coworkers but your prospects and customers as well. If you always show up with your homework done, I bet you'll find that, over time, your prospect can be counted on to show up with theirs done as well. If you always respond to emails on the same day, your prospect will start to do the same. We are wired to not let other people down, no matter if it's personal or professional. So your habits will make those around you better.

I love this quote by Jim Rohn: "Success is nothing more than a few simple disciplines practiced every day." So which parts of your success formula are you going to put on autopilot? What habits are you missing that you need to put in place to make sure they're there for you in the future? This goes back again to integrity or "Do the right things and the right things will happen." Build your success formula, be disciplined and do the work, then make sure the formula gets turned into habits, and as I shared earlier, you'll find by Year Three in the job, industry, or company, success comes easier and your place in the Top 10 Percent is within reach.

Make Your Process Repeatable and Pivot When Needed

Now that you understand the formula for success for *you* and you're building healthy habits to support your formula for success, the next step is to make sure it's repeatable while also recognizing when you need to make mid-course corrections or add a pivot to your process.

The only way to ensure that you stick to your formula for success is to make sure it's easy to execute. Building habits is one way to make things easier. But another is to give thought to when and how you can and should automate certain pieces of the formula.

Let's look at another Top 10 Percenter best practice: asking for referrals. Everyone knows you should do this, but very few sales reps actually have a process for doing so, and even fewer execute that process consistently. So, first, you'll build the process. Let's say your referral process looks something like this:

- Thirty days after the sale, you call the new client to make sure their onboarding went well.
- Forty-five days after the sale, you send an email with some best practice tips on how to get the most out of your product or service.
- Sixty days after the sale, you send an email sharing the details of your company's referral program that offers them incentives to referral new prospects to you.
- Sixty-three days after the sale, you call to ask for referrals to other people or companies that could benefit from your product.

Creating the process was the easy part; consistent execution will be the challenge. You need to ask yourself what pieces you can make repeatable or automate. Some examples:

- You need to create tasks for the four steps in the process listed above so you don't forget to do them in the timeframe in which they should be done. Referrals are more likely to happen within the first ninety days of someone buying because they are happy with their new shiny toy.

- You can create email templates for the emails you'll be sending. You can and should customize them before sending, but the meat of the email could be standardized.
- You can use an automation tool like HubSpot Sequences, Salesloft, or Outreach to trigger the emails and tasks automatically when it's time for them to be done.

If done correctly, you would be setting up the automation to start the countdown to Day Thirty right after you move a deal to Closed/Won.

What you've done here is take a key strategy within your formula for success and ensured that it happens for every deal you close in the same way at the same time—*each and every time.*

Here's another example straight out of my best practices playbook. I love doing discovery calls with my prospects, but I hate putting my notes in the CRM afterward. I know if I don't do it the same day, the chance of it happening is probably reduced by 20 percent each day after that. Due to my self-awareness of these tendencies and patterns, I built myself a "discovery call template" to make this task easier, which makes it more likely it will happen in a timely fashion. It has all the information I should know about my prospect and their company so I can determine if my consulting services would be a good fit to solve their issue. I love mine so much that I now create them for all my clients!

Here's a sample with some questions you should be asking yourself for each category:

Sample Discovery Call Template

Current Situation:

- What are they doing today?
- What's working?
- How many X do they have?
- How often does X need to be done?

Dept. Structure:

- How many employees in the department?
- What does the reporting structure look like?

Pain Point:

- What's not working?
- What issues are there with the current situation?

Impact of those pain points:

- How is this issue affecting the organization financially?
- What's the cost of not fixing that issue?

Buying Criteria:

- Issues that need solving to determine ROI:
- Business case confirmed:
- Point of differentiation:

Decision-Making Process:

- RFP (request for proposal) (Y/N):
- Committee decision (Y/N):
- Stakeholders:
- Contract Signer:

Budget:

- Is this a budgeted initiative?
- If so, what is the budget?
- How do non-budgeted initiatives get funded?

Fiscal Year:

- When is their fiscal year?
- When do they begin planning for the next fiscal year?

Competitors:

- Who else are they considering?
- What are the criteria the decision will be based on?

Education provided (Challenger):

- Industry standards:
- Best practices:

Handoff Notes for CSM

Now that I have all this juicy and valuable information on my prospect, I've also made it easier for me to send the follow-up email after the discovery call. Because of the consistent format of my discovery documentation, I've created a template for this email because I just copy and paste the information from the discovery template into the email template.

Here's the discovery follow-up email template I use:

Thank you {first name} for your time today and willingness to share so much information about your current situation and the challenges you and your team are currently facing.

Below is a summary of what I was able to gain from our conversation today.

- *Team:*
- *Current business situation:*
- *Challenges:*

- *Ideal solution:*
- *Next steps:*

I look forward to chatting again on X to review in detail how I would go about helping you solve the issues above.

Thank you again for your time and transparency around the current situation!

Kristie

Using my discovery follow up email template is especially important for me to use because I know part of my formula for success is "showing by example." What kind of credibility would I have as a sales consultant if I weren't using the same process I'm about to teach their sales team? I need to establish myself as a Top 10 Percenter before anyone will take me seriously or pay me what I'm worth. So I start to give them a little taste of what they can expect from their sales reps after I've finished working with them.

The key for me was to formalize and automate the strategies I know have helped me win clients in the past to make sure I repeat them with every prospect. You might have a different method for ensuring that you execute on your best practices consistently. The lesson here is personalizing the process so that it's easy and comfortable for you to execute.

want to caution you, however, not to fall into "I've always done it this way" and "It worked in the past" thinking. I'm all for being consistent with your success formula and the processes you build around it *until* it doesn't seem to be working anymore or isn't as effective. I do believe in mid-course correction and, when needed, a full-on pivot. These situations won't come up often, but when they do appear, you must recognize that a new method might be in order.

Here are a few situations that might cause you to change the processes you currently have in place to support your success formula.

- Your results aren't what they used to be.
- Your industry has had a major shift in how they buy. of a product or service like yours.
- Your company has made a pivot to selling to a different persona than you're currently selling to.
- Your company has expanded the offering into new verticals.
- New technology has come out that might yield better results (like using video to send your follow-ups instead of just regular email).
- A global pandemic occurs.

I'm not one to go looking for trouble where trouble doesn't need to exist (well, not that often anyway), so if it's working and you're happy and effective, then don't fix the unbroken. But as we all remember, no one saw a global pandemic on the horizon either, and the ability to pivot was what saved some companies from going out of business and some reps from losing their jobs during a very scary and uncertain time.

I'm going to suggest you now put this book down and write out your personal formula for success, a list of habits you know will support your formula, and a plan for how you can personalize and automate the process so you're more likely to stay on the path to success.

21

Being Generous with Your Overflow

As I wrote the founder's story for the beginning of this book, I was reminded yet again that my success was just as much the result of the support, mentorship, and love of so many people who've crossed my path throughout my career as it was about me working hard, doing the right things, and taking the right steps in my career. The reality that so many people cared about me and wanted to see me succeed is humbling, and I couldn't be more grateful.

Until I lost my job in 2016, I truly wasn't aware that so many people were in my corner and were cheering for me. The people who stepped forward to help me when I needed it had one thing in common; they are all Top 10 Percenters. They are all at the top of their game. They've made the money, bought the second home, and traveled to all the places on their bucket lists. Now they want to help others get there too.

But here's the other thing they have in common: they didn't wait until they'd made the money, bought the houses, and traveled the world to make themselves available to help others achieve success. They started helping others as they, too, were on their way to the top—not after they got there.

As I mentioned earlier, I met Mike Weinberg, famed author and speaker, almost by accident. I was in the process of interviewing for a VP of Sales position with a privately owned SaaS business when the Universe intervened, causing me to start the consulting business I own today. When it became clear to me I was on a collision course to consulting and a W2 job was no longer in my future, I reached out to the owners of the company I'd been interviewing with and shared that I would be heading down a different path, but that I thought that they should consider becoming my clients. They politely declined, and I wished them luck.

A week or so later, I received a call from one of the owners. Turned out they'd been using a local consultant, and they wanted me to meet with this person.

"Sure," I said. "I've got thirty minutes for everyone; who's the consultant?"

"Mike Weinberg," he said.

"Mike Weinberg, the author of *New Sales. Simplified.*?" I asked.

"Yes," he said.

I was shocked and curious.

Mike reached out a day later, and we set up a breakfast meeting. Admittedly, I was a little excited and nervous. Not only had I read Mike's book, but I had also used it as my team's quarterly book club book at previous sales leadership roles.

Mike and I hit it off right away. He was outgoing, funny, and engaged. I reviewed my sales leadership history and shared that I had decided to start my consulting career just as he had several years earlier. He was excited and supportive of me and my decision. I told him I thought the company he was consulting for should hire me as their Fractional VP of Sales, but they had turned me down.

"Don't worry," he said. "I'll talk to them."

A few days later, I was invited back in to discuss how the fractional sales leader position would work and hammer out the details. I ended up helping that company for a year.

But that was just a small part of the support I received from Mike as I forged into the new world of owning a business. Over the next year, Mike helped me figure out how to charge for my services, shared his consulting agreement with me, regularly met with me in person to provide support, answered any questions I had or challenges I faced, and, most importantly, helped me work through my imposter syndrome. All of this occurred during what I call his "breakout year." Mike's second book, *Sales Management. Simplified*, had just been released a few months earlier, and Mike was on his way to being the sought-after speaker and consultant he is today.

I'm eternally grateful that Mike showed up in my life when he did. I'm certain I would have figured things out eventually through trial and error, but having Mike help me steer my early career in the right direction in the first few months saved me the pain of making as many mistakes as I would have and helped me hit the ground running faster, allowing for success much earlier than it might otherwise have happened.

That's just one of the many stories about how I've been on the receiving end of someone being generous with their overflow. But the truth is that I've benefited every bit as much by being the person who chose to be generous and share overflow with others.

Even before I lost my job and started my consulting business, I said to anyone who reached out for help, "Sure! I've got thirty minutes for everyone." And I still mean it when I say it today. For years, I've been reviewing and editing resumes for friends, family, and strangers. I often spend thirty minutes giving career advice to those who are in a rut, are looking to pivot, or need help negotiating a job offer. I mentor for a nonprofit organization that helps startup founders take their idea from a side hustle to a $10M company.

I'm not saying all this to brag. I'm telling you this because having thirty minutes for everyone not only brings me joy and lets me make so many serendipitous and meaningful connections, I also believe it's my responsibility to pay it forward for all the support and kindness I've been afforded by those who have their own jobs, families, and lives and still took time to help, support, and guide me.

So, as you're on your way to the top, I'm challenging you to find ways to support others who aren't as far along in their journey as you are. You will have a wide variety of opportunities to give back as you continue to climb to the top of your sales career.

Mentor a New Rep

Being the new kid on the block is scary. They're trying to figure out, in the shortest time possible, the new boss, new company, new industry, and probably a new sales process and strategy. It's a lot for a new sales rep to wrap their hands and head around.

You can make this transition easier. You already know the lay of the internal land at your company. You've figured out how to manage your boss, what the internal politics are like, and what the culture is like. Share what you've learned, maybe at lunch, with your new coworkers as they try to navigate their way in their new environment.

Because you also understand the industry and sales process, offer to let them sit in on discovery calls to help them learn the questions they need to ask to qualify a prospect. Or invite them to go along for an in-person meeting or presentation so they can see how you present the solution to a group of decision-makers.

Taking a new employee under your wing will not only help them get up and running faster, but it will also help you polish your skills. Teaching is a great reminder of the tasks you're doing that have made you successful and also a great way to refine the way you do those tasks to create even greater success.

Volunteer

Volunteer to share your business knowledge with those still in school who don't know much about sales or business. Sales isn't taught in high school, and only around 150 universities offer a degree in sales, but statistics show that around 50 percent of college grads' initial jobs will be in sales. You can help them better prepare for a job in sales by sharing your experience and knowledge.

I started teaching for Junior Achievement (JA) over fifteen years ago as the result of frustration around the lack of financial literacy I saw all around me. As I mentioned earlier in the book, I was lucky enough to have been raised in a family that openly talked about money, expenses, and investing. But I quickly realized as I got older that most people are extremely undereducated on the topic of finances.

I chose JA for two reasons--initially, because my dad had also taught for JA, and if Dad thought it was a good way to help, then I was sure he was right. But as I went through training to be a JA instructor, I also realized that every lesson at every grade level had a financial component to it. From "Your Community" for second graders where they get to run their own business and use the money from their business to buy goods and services from their store owner classmates, to "International Business" that discusses tariffs and trade agreements, JA is an amazing organization that has numerous programs to help give students a glimpse into the business world, which they might not otherwise be exposed to.

There are so many other ways you can give your time and share your sales expertise with kids who just aren't sure what they want to be when they grow up or what their options even are. Look around to see how you might help put a child on the path to a future sales career.

Be a Resource

Just like my "I have thirty minutes for everyone" mentality, you, too, can be a resource for friends, family members, and strangers in your life. You've developed skills and have had experiences that others around you would benefit from knowing about and learning from.

Offer to do a mock interview, review a resume, or help develop questions with someone who is prepping for an important job interview. You know what sales hiring managers are looking for and need to hear to feel comfortable when hiring a new sales rep.

You also understand what options are out there under the sales umbrella. Help a friend or the child of a friend understand the difference between a hunter and farmer or between an inside and outside sales rep. The sales world is confusing, and there are so many options to choose from.

As you reach the top of your profession or the end of your career, think back to all those people who helped you along the way. The people who gave you advice, were there to pick you up when you fell, lent an ear when you'd lost the big sale, or always came to the game with their pom poms at the ready. You didn't get to the top by yourself; no one does. Some of those people who passed through your life had a starring role, like Carl did for me. Others maybe played a bit part, like my manager, David, who told me when I was 26 that I needed to be more willow than oak—that advice was timely then and is still a helpful reminder today.

I encourage you to give thought to how you can be the person who makes a difference in the life of someone just starting their career in sales, who has had a career setback, as I did, or who just needs to hear they're a Rock Star when they miss quota. Your years of experience, wisdom, and connections could make a difference in the life and success of someone you might not even know today. And I guarantee that being generous with your overflow will make a huge difference in your life and success as well.

22

Making the Right Moves at the Right Time

Now that you've done the work to understand what drives you, how you like to be rewarded, what the right sales role is for you, what your strengths you'll turn into your sales secret weapon, and what swim lane you should stay in, you're making better decisions about how to position yourself for success, where to put your focus and your energy, and how to negotiate for the benefits that really matter to you. By this point your day to day should not only be easier, it should also be more rewarding.

Now, it's all about making the right moves at the right time. Of course, that will depend on things like the stage you're in within your sales career, the industry and sales role you're in, and your short- and long-term goals, but it also depends on how you want to position yourself in your field.

Position Yourself as an Elite Sales Professional

By the three-year mark, you've racked up enough experience and time in the field to position yourself as one of the elites, the Top 10 Percent of talent in your industry or region. This positioning is based on more than your sales record; hiring professionals will look for indications that you're ambitious, strategic, and savvy about your career trajectory.

I recently listened to a podcast interview with Mark Lore, founder of Diapers.com and Jet.com. Amazon bought Diapers.com for $545M, and Walmart purchased Jet.com for a cool $3.3B. All told, Marc's companies have netted him over $4B. Although the entire podcast was fascinating, I was most interested in Marc's discussion about how he hires "elite" sales talent—the Top 5 Percent of performers. He not only focuses on making sure he hires the Top 5 Percent of talent for his company, he makes sure the companies he invests in also build a team of Top 5 Percenters. Here's what he had to say:

"You can't hire people just because you'd like to have a beer with them. Unconscious bias is real, and you must stay objective."

Here's what Marc looks for on a resume:

- Where did they start their career after college?
- Did they get promoted while they were there?
- When they left that first job and moved to their next job, is that next move one a Top 5 Percenter would make? (He says Top 5 Percenters move in a certain way that's very strategic—a bigger title, a much bigger role, or a better company.)
- While at that company, how many times did they get promoted?
- How many times have they made a big "step-change?"

Any deviation from that progression on a resume, and he won't even interview them for fear he will like them and that unconscious bias will cause him to hire an average player. So what did I find so fascinating about how he determines if they are a 5 Percenter?

- Elite talent thinks differently and, as a result, acts differently than average talent.
- Career progression matters.
- To be the best, you need to work for the best, challenge yourself, and put yourself in a position to outperform the other 95 percent.

It might seem like there is a little magic at play here, but it's just practical. I look for the same things Marc does; I just describe them differently.

Your Decisions Aren't Just about Advancement Strategies; They Have to Match Your Personal Goals

The next thing you need to think about as you decide how long to stay at a company or what next move will be the right one for you is your personal short- and long-term goals. Usually, your short-term goals are a means to an end, the end being your long-term goals.

Let's say your long-term goal is to retire at fifty-two with a vacation home, the ability to travel several times a year, and to be debt-free. At some point, you'll probably need to find your "last" job that will take you down the home stretch, but in the short-term, you need to choose opportunities that will teach you new skills, help you connect and network with the "right" people, and put you in a place to not only choose your last job but allow you to write your own ticket—the ticket that takes you all the way to "home base."

Short-term goals are ones you plan to achieve in the next twelve to eighteen months, and they're really just the building blocks of your long-term goal. These are goals you need to accomplish to put yourself a step closer to the goal of selling your way into the life you want while you're still working and after you retire.

Several years ago, I decided I wanted to make a *big* step-change from a small privately-owned company to a publicly held company in the same industry. I had a relationship with several executives at the company of my dreams and secured an interview for an available position to run their EMEA division. I spent hours preparing for the interview. I did extensive research on the company, talked with everyone I had a relationship with there, and polished my resume until it shone. I was confident as I flew to the East Coast on the big day. I'd spent eight years in this industry; I was a subject matter expert, well-respected in the space, and as prepared as I'd ever been for an interview. This job was mine to lose.

And that's exactly what happened. I got the call a few days after, and the hiring manager agreed with me that I had amazing experience, knew my sh*t had great relationships, and would be a great cultural fit. The one thing I didn't have? International experience. I hadn't considered that not having worked or sold internationally would be a huge disadvantage for the company.

I was devastated but not deterred. My long-term goal for working for that company was on hold, for now. I needed to put a short-term goal in place that would ensure I wouldn't be rejected in the future. Two years later, I got an opportunity to run the Canadian division of a CPG (consumer packaged goods) company. Marc Lore would probably say it was a "weird" step-change to leave software and work for a CPG company, but it checked a box I hoped would put me back on the right path to work for my dream company, so I took it. It was not only a short-term goal to get international experience, but it was also short-lived. I got the experience I needed and jumped right back into software twelve months later.

Three years after I was rejected from my dream company, I got another opportunity to interview there, this time for a channel partner position. I've told you the story of meeting the hiring manager in Chicago and being interviewed over coffee at the Midway airport. I got a call a couple of days later with a generous offer, which much to everyone's surprise, I respectfully turned down. After spending a couple of hours with my future boss, I realized he was just biding his time until he could retire, and I knew he wouldn't help me be a better leader, person, or executive. It wasn't the right next step at this point in my career. And when the friend who already worked for this boss asked me in disbelief, "Why would you turn that down?" I just said, "I want a mentor, not just a boss. He isn't going to make me better." Although we were both disappointed, he knew I was doing the right thing for my career.

Sometimes the company is right, but the opportunity is wrong. This opportunity wasn't aligned with my long-term goal of working for a boss who would challenge me and invest in my professional growth. So that position might have been a great match for my short-term goals, but it would have sidelined my long-term goal of learning from the best and growing exponentially in every position I accepted.

When Is Staying Put Actually the Right Move?

Sometimes, you just need to stay long enough for your life to get easier and to reap the fruits of your labor. Sometimes, moving on would be throwing away the greatest opportunity you could ever have.

There is no better example of this than with my brother, Scott. Scott has been a senior account executive with his current company in the staffing industry for twenty-five years now. He joined the company a year out of college as a recruiter and, within a couple of years, was promoted to account executive and assigned what was one of the largest telecommunication accounts in the country. It took him a year to get a handle on the lay of the land at this Fortune 500 account.

Staffing is extremely competitive, so you must build strong relationships with HR, the hiring managers, and top executives at the company if you want to beat out the competition and make sure the candidates you present to the company have an advantage. As a member of the engineering division of his company, Scott had to learn all about the skill sets of an engineer as well as the culture and nuances of the telecommunications company. He needed to make sure when he presented a candidate that not only did they have the skills needed to do the job, but they would also fit the environment and work well with the manager and other team members.

After spending five years learning the ins and outs of the telecommunications industry, he transitioned out of that account and was assigned an account in the automotive industry. With knowledge of engineering already under his belt, he only needed to learn about the auto industry and how their engineering needs might differ from the telecommunications industry. But that was the easy part. The hard part was working to build relationships with a whole new set of stakeholders, starting at zero! This is just like being transferred to a new city and trying to build a new territory from scratch—not easy.

He started in HR and worked to meet each person who had responsibility for hiring and staffing the 7,000-employee plant. Over the past eighteen years, he has developed a strong working relationship with the VP of HR and has come to understand her hiring criteria and what type of candidates to present to have the best chance at getting a placement. He grew that account over the next several years to the point where he was exceeding his quota consistently year after year. In the past twenty-five years, he's made President's Club eighteen times and has been the top producer in his region two out of the past three years.

The current standard for job longevity in sales is 4.6 years, according to the Bureau of Labor and Statistics in 2018. (Under three years if you're a Zillennial, my word for the millennial and Gen Z groups.) When Scott and I discussed his longevity in comparison to those statistics, I asked if he believed he'd be where he is today if he'd taken a new job every three to five years. He was adamant that he knew he wouldn't be. In fact, he feels strongly that if you're in the right role, selling a good product, and working for a good company, leaving before the five-year mark is when reps leave the most money on the table. "Starting over, if you're in sales, at a certain point doesn't make professional or financial sense," he said. "You work hard to build trust, relationships, and your territory. Starting a new job and starting at zero reduces your ability to maximize your income. Maybe that works for other professions," he said, "but not if you're in sales."

Even in such a specialized field, Scott would agree that you can build consistent business in your first three years. But he'd also tell you that his goal was never to just build consistent business; his ultimate goal was to get *exclusive* business. That can take five years or more, but in his words, "Getting exclusive business, eliminating your competition altogether, is when the windfall happens."

Having "grown up" in the software world where the average tenure at a company in Silicon Valley is under two years, I tend to agree. I saw good sales reps walk away from great jobs at great companies with hefty stock options just to go to work for the newest cool kid company on the block.

It was shocking to me. I also noticed the Gen Xers were more likely to stay put, and it almost always benefited them financially.

As we've discussed in earlier chapters, you may need to try out a few different types of sales positions to figure out what your sales swim lane is. No one expects you to stay twenty years at the first sales job you take. You may have three positions in your first six to seven years in sales, and these could all be at the same company, or they might be at a couple of different companies. I encourage you to try a few different sales positions on for size, early in your career, to find the right fit for you.

At the beginning of your sales career, moving around a bit is to be expected and won't be frowned upon by hiring managers and sales leaders, so don't be afraid to change positions if you get into a situation where you aren't being provided formal and ongoing sales training, aren't passionate about the product or service you're selling, or are feeling there is a cultural mismatch between you and the company.

But after you figure out where you can leverage your sales secret weapon and have settled into the swim lane that lets you be successful and financially rewarded, then it might be time to double down and maximize that current opportunity. Remember my three-year rule: sales jobs get easier in Year Three. That's when all your hard work to understand the product, industry, and your competitors starts to pay off. You also put in the time prospecting and working deals through the sales cycle, and it's in Year Three those NRNs will start to resurface (if you've properly nurtured them). So maximize each position at every stage in your sales career to set you up for success when you make the next step-change.

"It Depends." Taking Your Industry and Role into Consideration

The last thing to consider when deciding "should you stay or should you go" is the industry you're in and the sales role you have. Think about my brother's situation. Staffing is a relationship business, and you keep what you catch, so it doesn't make sense to move around a lot after you've worked hard to build relationships with your clients and built a rolodex of qualified candidates you know you can count on to overperform at the next contract position that comes open. Working for five staffing companies over ten years will most likely negatively impact your income potential.

On the other hand, if you're a pure hunter who starts at zero each month, it might not be as risky to leave your $50M company to go hunt for a $560M company where the average sale is ten times what you're currently selling.

You have to consider your industry and how the relationships you've built might play into your long-term goals and success before deciding to jump ship. The same is true for the *type* of sales position you have. If you are working on 100 percent commission and repeat business is everything, then you must consider the lost time and opportunity of leaving established relationships. If you're in a role where you pass your newly sold clients onto an account manager or customer success manager to grow and nurture, then relationships may have less impact on your ability to #ownyourownincome.

The last thing I want to mention regarding things to consider before you jump ship is about burning bridges and ticking off the wrong people. I strongly believe it's my responsibility as a leader to make you better and be there to support you if you choose to take a different path or position with another company. As someone who made career steps to better my financial and professional position, I understand and respect those who feel they've learned all they needed to from the job they're in and need to move on to advance their career.

With that said, there is a right way and a wrong way to move on. The right way is to give plenty of notice, present your former boss and company in a good light during future conversations, and continue to be an advocate for the industry and company, when you can. Most industries are smaller than you think, and you won't want a poor exit to ruin your chances of bettering yourself in the future.

And who knows? You might someday be back at the company you're leaving.

23

Knowing Yourself Is a Shortcut to Success

At the beginning of this book, I discussed two defining experiences I had that led me to sales leadership—waiting tables and the "MBA" I received at my family's kitchen table every night. Those experiences put me on my path, but the experiences I had after that are what kept me moving in the right direction.

I started my career immediately out of college in retail sales management. I spent eight years there, beginning as a department manager in a regional department store and then advancing to be a buyer for a major retailer. Most people thought my job sounded super fun and glamorous, traveling to New York monthly to decide what women in the Midwest would be wearing next season.

I wish! The buyer job was fun (at first) but not glamorous, just challenging. My performance was reviewed on revenue and gross margin, so the job was more math than modern fashion. I quickly learned analytical skills and how to be a shrewd negotiator (bargaining with Marty at Mudd over the cost of denim shorts was no easy task!).

The way to win at the retail game as a buyer was simple. The buyer with the fewest markdowns wins. This required that you had the right assortment of items in the right stores, at the right time. By assortment, I mean the right color of short-sleeved top, enough of the right sizes, and delivered just in time for seventy-degree weather. This challenge didn't require that I have any fashion sense—just common sense and a good calculator.

As I was entering my eighth year in retail, a couple of things happened that moved me in a new direction. I began my career as a buyer in the Juniors department, buying denim, dresses, and swimwear. It was the perfect starter buying gig. Junior consumers are picky and cost-conscious, so if you bought the "right" items, they moved quickly, and you would need to order more asap and have them shipped as soon as you could. I loved buying for this age group. They were fashion-forward with flair, and as far as revenue contribution and risk were concerned, a new buyer for the Juniors department was considered to be really low risk. So this position came with a lot of autonomy and authority, which of course, I loved!

I experienced a bit of a system shock when I was promoted to the plus-sized Better Women's clothing. It was the anti-Junior department. Better Women's clothing was much higher priced and *way* more conservative. It was also a much more visible department because of the amount of revenue the Better Women's total clothing division brought in, which also included missy and petite sizes.

I felt the differences right away. The first difference I noticed was that the GMM (general merchandise manager), whom I hardly remember meeting while I was a buyer in the Junior's department, was very involved in all aspects of the business. The second difference was a pleasant surprise—the vendors in this space—Liz Claiborne, Tommy Hilfiger, and Jones New York—had much bigger entertainment budgets, so trips to New York became events filled with Broadway shows and really nice dinners.

But two things that became obvious over the next few months made me question my career direction and ultimately convinced me I needed to take a sharp right turn and not look back.

The first thing was that I started to feel like a grown-up banned to the kids table at Thanksgiving. As a result of buying for more visible brands, each time the three buyers in Better Women's clothing went to New York, we would have a twenty-person meeting with each vendor. These meetings included me, my buyer counterparts buying the other sizes, my boss, my counterparts' bosses, and their boss, the GMM. Oh, and sometimes the president of the department store joined us as well.

On the vendor side, the roster looked about the same. The executives would talk among themselves, attempting to negotiate the best price for their team, as my coworkers and I sat there with our laptops open, trying to look like we were participating. I understood this was above my pay grade (there was discount power in numbers), but it was making the job less fun.

The second thing that happened challenged my integrity and value system. As noted earlier, markdowns were the bane of our existence as buyers. What the general public doesn't understand is that not only does the department store take a financial hit on clothes that need to be discounted because they've been on the rack too long, but the vendor also chips in to help cover the financial loss since they were the ones that decided to manufacture that ugly pattern to begin with!

So, every month, buyers are required to negotiate markdown money from each vendor to help cover the cost of marking down the slow-selling items. Then, on the last day of each month, you turn in the "markdown money" you collected from your vendors so the financial reports can be completed.

I was already getting disenchanted with my life as a buyer when I got a call on the last day of the month from my boss. He said, "I need you to write up markdown money in the amount of $X for vendor Y."

I was confused and replied, "I didn't negotiate X amount of markdown money with vendor Y."

"Just write it up and bring it to me for signature," he said.

Wow! What was going on here? This was a man I liked and respected. What was he really asking me to do? I did as instructed and walked down the hall to his office and entered with a look of confusion and concern.

"What's going on?" I asked as I handed the document over to him for signature.

"Take this to accounting," he said after signing it.

I'm a rules girl. Despite my sassy personality, I'm not usually one to break the rules. But I did as I was told and left for the weekend. I came in on Monday with little memory of the incident from Friday—until the phone rang and again my boss was on the other end. This time he told me I needed to write up a markdown reversal and bring it down for signature. Not sure that I had heard him correctly, not to mention the fact I didn't even know there was a markdown reversal form, I asked him to repeat himself. Yep, I'd heard him right; we were going to reverse the money we'd put through on Friday.

Well, now it was time to do some digging. I walked across the hall to a more senior buyer I trusted and gingerly broached the situation that seemed to be unfolding in my business. She confirmed that she, too, had been asked to do the same on Friday and again this morning.

"What do you think is going on?" I asked. Her best guess was the company was having financial issues and needed to hit a month-end number to report to Wall Street. I just stared at her in disbelief. Not only was this wrong, but I was also pretty sure it was illegal. This was a head-on collision between my paycheck and my integrity. My boss and my boss's boss were people I looked up to, respected, and liked. The realization of what was going on was devastating. It would be impossible to ever look at them the same way again. Unsure about how to handle the fuzzy accounting I was being asked to participate in, I continued to do my job and keep a close eye on the discussions being had and the decisions being made.

As the next month was coming to a close, I received another call from my boss identical to the one I'd received the month before. I did as instructed and walked down the hall, which now seemed much longer than it had just thirty days ago. I handed the paper to my boss for signature, and he looked at the piece of paper and then back at me and said, "You haven't signed this." To which I replied, "And I won't be. I didn't negotiate this, and I'm not saying I did." He signed it, leaving the box for my signature blank, and handed it back to me to deliver to accounting.

At this point, I was painfully aware that my time in retail was coming to an end. The very next day, I dusted off my resume and updated it in preparation for beginning the search for my next chapter. I was so disturbed about what had happened that I made the decision to not only leave retail as an industry but also that my days working for a publicly traded company were over as well. If this is what happens at Fortune 500 companies, I decided, I'll pass.

After making the decision to leave my old career behind me, I spent some time thinking about what the next chapter should look like. This was a major step-change, and I needed to be careful and thoughtful about how I approached the next chapter. After giving it a lot of consideration, I decided the theme for my next step was this: "I'm looking for a company, not a job."

I'd developed a lot of different skills over the past eight years in retail— people leadership, analytical skills, and negotiation skills—and I didn't want to go in search of a "title." I wanted an environment that would take my existing skills to the next level and add to them. Knowing that I wanted the right company and wasn't going to be hung up on a title, I needed to decide what type of company would be right for me to learn what I wanted to learn to set me up for the next step.

It was easier to start with the type of company I didn't want. Based on my prior experience, I knew I didn't want a large or publicly owned company. Been there, done that. I wanted a smaller company, where I'd learn various facets of the business and have a seat with the Knights of the Round Table.

During this time of transition, I got together for drinks with a current coworker and our former boss, who had been the DMM (divisional merchandise manager) before our current boss. As we sat around discussing my decision to leave retail, an interesting conversation ensued.

I shared my strategy of looking for a company and not a position, and I could see the confusion on their faces. Finally, my former boss spoke up for both of them. "I can't believe you're leaving retail. What other industry do you think your skills will be transferable to?"

Now I was the one with a look of confusion. It was obvious to me. "We have so many valuable skills that we've learned and honed as buyers," I told them. "We have strong analytical skills, negotiation skills, leadership skills, and we're required to balance our books once a week. Those skills would be valuable to so many companies."

They were skeptical. They only thought of themselves as merchandisers and buyers, specific job roles, not as people with a multitude of skills and talents. I knew I had much more to give, and more to the point, I knew every job I'd had up to that point, from waitressing to giving private racquetball lessons, and to retail, had only added to my list of transferable skills and assets I would be bringing to my next opportunity.

You've already "met" Dean Pichee, so you're probably guessing just how pivotal this point was for me. As I started to network, one of the first people I had coffee with was Dean, who owned a software company with around twelve employees. Dean was running his second company after selling his first company to a competitor. As a transplant to St. Louis, where being "homegrown" is so important that the first question people ask you when you meet is, "Where did you go to high school?" I knew it would be important to network with someone who grew up here. When Dean and I met for coffee, I was hopeful he would hand out my resume (remember—it was the year 2000; paper was still in fashion) to all his other business-owner friends.

I checked in with Dean a couple of weeks later to see who he'd given my resume to that I should be following up with. "Well," he said, "no one." That was disappointing. "But," he added, "I think we should meet again. I might have something for you." Intrigued, I agreed.

Over lunch, Dean said he had plans to grow the company and was considering hiring an HR manager and thought maybe I would be a good fit for that position. I do not have a poker face, so I know my nonverbal communication was obvious. I laughed and told him we obviously hadn't spent enough time together because that was a horrible idea and he'd end up firing me within six months. At thirty, I knew myself well enough to know I didn't possess the traits needed to be a successful HR manager.

We parted ways again that day, and I was hopeful he would talk me up to his friends, and soon I would be meeting with other small business owners who might benefit from my skill set. But a week later, he called and wanted to meet for lunch again. He was upping the ante. After we'd ordered, he got right into it. "I parted ways with a partner a few months ago, and I need someone with business experience to help me grow the business. I like your business skills, and I think the company and I would benefit from having someone more mature with your background and ambition."

Well, okay then. This was better than trying my hand at HR and maybe better than him giving my resume to people he knew but who didn't know me. "What would the role look like?" I asked.

"I'm not sure," he said. "I just know I need help, and I don't have anyone as experienced as you on my staff currently."

There was something enticing and adventurous about taking a bit of a blind faith leap into a whole new world. Over the next ten years, I helped Dean take the company from under $2M to over $8M and from fifteen employees to fifty. I went from following him around like a puppy for the first two weeks, not having a clue what I'd gotten myself into, to being responsible for the entire company's revenue in a few years.

Over those ten years, I got the equivalent of a PhD in SaaS software sales, hiring and firing, leading and inspiring commissioned reps, and I had a front-row seat at how a business owner makes tactical and strategic business decisions. It was exactly what I said I wanted when I started out. A company that would value my existing skills and force me to add new ones while giving me a seat at the big kids' table.

It was the right time in my growth cycle to take a major step-change. I was young enough to be able to take the risk, knowing if it didn't work out that I could recover, and it wouldn't have an irreversible impact on my long-term career goals. More important than that, I was starting to really know myself. I understood the skills I had developed, thanks to my eight years in retail. While my other retailer coworkers thought of themselves only as merchandisers and retailers and didn't believe they had anything to offer another industry, I knew I wasn't a title or an industry. I was a set of skills that were valued in a lot of different roles and companies. I had also had my integrity challenged, and if I found myself in that situation in the future, I would know what to do.

Self-awareness is a superpower. The better you know yourself, your values, your skills, and ultimately your worth, the easier it will be to achieve the success you dream of. It allows you to understand what makes you tick, what motivates you, and why you make the decisions you make (good and bad). When you understand all those things, you'll also know when it's time to make a step-change that will take your career to the next level.

The sooner you can see the vision you have for your life, including what you will and won't put up with or live without, the faster and easier it will be to see the right opportunities at the right time. I knew I wouldn't compromise my integrity or values for that company or any company. I also knew I wanted my voice to be heard and a seat with the Knights of the Round Table. This is one of the reasons I gravitated toward working for and helping startups. Working for smaller companies in fast-growth mode ensures that my voice is heard and my contribution matters.

Earlier in the book, I told you a story about Brent and how I had seen a skill that he hadn't yet identified in himself. Although he hadn't understood he had strong sales skills, his willingness to try new things and take a bit of risk paid off with a VP title. I planted the seed, but Brent was willing, when the time came, to see this step-change as the possible long-term career opportunity it did, in fact, turn out to be. Brent had been at the company a year and a half when he was approached about moving from the development team to the sales team. The decision to make a major shift in departments was made easier as a result of the trust he had in the leadership and his love for the company. If it hadn't worked out, the company would have transferred him back to the development team, and he really wouldn't have lost much ground. It was the right time to make a step-change, and Brent was self-aware enough to understand the risk was low but the upside was huge!

Of course, having self-awareness and really knowing yourself and what you want increases your chances of making the right decisions at the right time, but it doesn't guarantee that you won't make a misstep. It just means you're more likely to recognize that misstep quickly, allowing you to make a mid-course correction.

I openly share with people that I've made all the right steps, with one exception. I mentioned in the last chapter that not having international experience caused me to lose the position I wanted with my dream company, and I'd had a short stint with a CPG company that afforded me that international experience I lacked. What I didn't share was how wrong I had been about the company where I chose to get that international experience.

As I read the job description on the LinkedIn posting, I was intrigued and a bit excited. The CPG company was VC-backed, with top-tier executives who had just turned around another struggling CPG company. Most importantly I would be leading the sales team in Canada. I know, it wasn't Europe or Asia, but I definitely needed my passport to go to Canada, so it qualified as "international."

What I hadn't factored in, because I didn't know what I didn't know, was that CPG is not anything like software sales. And this wasn't even CPG as I thought of it, blush and bleach and the like; this was in the food industry. And not the people food industry. This was dog and cat food. Oh, boy. Let the games begin.

I knew I wasn't in Kansas anymore when I sat in on my first distribution meeting where it was announced that we weren't currently able to produce dog food X because of a shortage of the secret ingredient that made it so special. What? We were at a work stoppage due to a missing ingredient? All I could think was when we needed to build a new software feature, the determining factor was how soon it needed to be built, and that determined how many developers we threw at the project. Now, we were talking about being out of stock on product and how to communicate that to the distributors. Yikes!

As I affectionately say about those ten long months I spent in the industry, dog food isn't sexy, and it's not software. I was keenly aware by month three that I'd made a misstep, and I began to plot my exit, but not before I got that passport stamped a few times over the coming months. I knew I needed to explain to the next hiring manager the reason I not only took a CPG job but also the reason I only stayed ten months, so I made sure I had a story to tell. I wanted to check that international experience box on my resume. And in those ten months, I had done just that.

What do I want you to learn from these stories? Simply put, every experience is part of a whole. If I look at each of those stories by themselves, they're just a series of successes and failures. But if I look at them as clues, I learn what matters most to me, what works best for me, and what decisions and moves I need so I can win more and lose less.

The two most important things you'll ever learn about your career are 1. what you really want to get out of it and 2. what you won't put up with. By looking at all of my choices and experiences as pieces of the puzzle, I've been able to continually and exponentially sell my way into the life I have, which is only getting better all the time. And I've taught others to look at their own choices and experiences in the same way, which gives me the joy of celebrating with people like Becky and Brent and so many more who are selling their way into the life they want as well.

Paying attention to these clues and solving the "puzzle of you" is a shortcut to #ownyourownincome. Because the better you know yourself and the life and career you're carving out, the faster you'll be able to identify when you've taken a left turn. In the same way that Becky learned the importance of autonomy and structure and Matt learned how much he valued variety and challenge, and I learned that I loved sexy, fast-developing, even high-risk roles but wouldn't tolerate anything that rubs my morals the wrong way, you'll learn what matters most and what won't work for you at all. The sooner you take yourself out of an unworkable situation that will end in misery and put yourself into a workable situation that will lead to success, the better.

24

Close the Skill Gap

The same process of looking at your experiences as clues to learning about yourself will help you define gaps in your skill set or experience. For instance, I often work with reps who have mastered the art of doing discovery. They are skilled at asking the right big-picture, open-ended questions and then drilling down further to uncover the pain the prospect and company are feeling. They are in complete control of the prospect and the sales cycle early on. Their ability to be in control of the conversation and prospect early in the sales cycle sets them up for great success, but as the sales cycle drags on, I see a shift in control. I refer to this as "abdicating the sales cycle to the prospect."

After the sales rep has identified how their company and solution will solve the prospect's issues, the prospect then needs to talk to others, get budget approval, or get approval from the board. At this point, control seems to slowly and seamlessly shift to the prospect as the cycle starts to move at a pace that's more comfortable for them. The sales rep feels they don't have control over the timeline at this point and calls just to "check in" and see if any progress has been made. No longer are firm, scheduled calls on the calendar with structured agendas intended to move the sales cycle forward. Eventually, the deal goes cold and is moved to the Closed/ Lost stage.

It's hard for reps to understand and accept that they can keep control of the sales cycle throughout the entire process, but those who do identify this as a missing skill or weakness are the ones that go on to be Top 10 Percenters.

Another missing skill the 90 percent are missing is the ability to transform an internal champion into a temporary sales rep. In a large percentage of deals, you won't be present when the discussion and decision regarding whether or not to purchase your product/service happens, but your internal champion will be. The Top 10 Percenters understand they need to spend time with their champion, helping them prepare to present the business case, handle objections, and go for the close in front of the buying committee. Top 10 Percenters understand that abdicating that role to an underprepared champion is setting both of them up for failure.

The ability to identify missing experience to open the door to your next opportunity is just as critical as identifying gaps in your skill set. Although I still consider my short-lived time at the CPG company a misstep, it was my realization that not having international experience on my resume might limit my career path that made me take the step-change I did, and because that was my primary objective, I still consider it a successful move in the bigger picture.

The biggest gap in experience I find as a result of my work with startup founders is the lack of sales and marketing experience because most founders come from a technology or development background. It's not realistic for them to step away from their role of CEO/founder for twelve to eighteen months while they get that missing experience at another company, but they can put sales and marketing experts on their board, hire sales and marketing consultants, read sales/marketing books, or listen to podcasts. I recently had an opportunity to work with a Midwestern startup where I was one of three consultants on the payroll at the same time. I was working on the sales process and strategy; another consultant was trying to undo the over-customized CRM system while adding reports and dashboards, and the third consultant was helping HR build a formal interview process and put together career paths for each department.

What impressed me the most was the founder's self-awareness around what his core competencies were and what needed to be outsourced to ensure the long-term success of the company.

It's the ability to identify and acknowledge these gaps in your skill set or experience that will help you quickly adjust and seek out training, mentorship, or a new challenge to help you fill those gaps and ensure you can stay on the path to success you've planned.

Truly knowing yourself and updating that knowledge base with every experience and outcome can be the professional hack you need to shorten your path to success. The sooner you understand things like your non-negotiables (including things tied to your character and values), your sales sweet spot, your professional secret weapons, what swim lane you perform best in, the skills you have that are transferable to other positions and companies, and the gaps in your skills set that still need to be developed, the more likely you'll be able to reduce the amount of time it takes to reach the level of success you're looking for.

25

Time for an Audit

We've covered a lot of ground as we've woven our way from my early years at the family dinner table with my brother and me earning our sales MBA equivalents, through uncovering strengths and secret weapons you didn't know you had, to turning those strengths into your personal formula for selling your way into whatever you want, and finally to asking you to use what you've learned and accomplished to help others achieve their goals.

Through all the stories, suggestions, and sales advice, the one message I hope has really resonated with you is that you have choices. You have choices regarding how you earn a living and about the type of sales roles you take, the industries you sell into, the companies you work for, and the leaders you learn from. More than that, you have choices about how you develop your strengths and habits, and how you #sowtogrow to keep advancing your goals and your career.

Let's do a little review and an "audit" of your steps for positioning yourself to join the Rock Star 10 Percenters.

I hope you took the time to really look inward and were honest with yourself about what drives you, what empowers you, what your reward structure is, and what will bring you to tears. Understanding these things will help you make choices about the sales superpowers you want to hone, how you want to build mental memory, the choice of using positive self-talk versus negative self-talk, the choice to use visualization techniques, the choice of a swim lane, and the choice to do the right thing every time the opportunity comes up.

I also hope you've taken the choice to #ownyourownshit to heart. That you've recognized that blaming others for your choices, your struggles, or your results won't ever put you in the Top 10 Percent.

If you've not built a circle of like-minded, successful, and supportive people, make that priority number one. The difference that having people in your life makes will challenge you to continually up your game and could be the difference between being in the Top 10 Percent and being the other 90 percent.

I've seen this firsthand in the company my brother keeps. His circle is made up of mostly high school and college friends, and in the summer, the lake friends. What do they all have in common? They're all Top 10 Per-centers in their respective fields—finance, wealth management, concrete, catering, health care, and more. No two of them are in the same industry or have taken the same career path, but when they're drinking a beer on the boat at Stockton Lake or getting eighteen holes in at Big Cedar Lodge, they're always talking shop and making each other better in the process.

The next thing I'd like to see you do is take an honest look at your current position and ask yourself if it is really a stepping stone to where you want to be, or is it maybe the next step-change that will put you on the path? Have you overstayed your welcome? Are you too comfortable? Is the product you're selling not keeping up with the competition? Is your industry having an identity crisis? Is your sales leader making you a better salesperson and person? I'm not advocating for you to hand your resignation letter to your boss tomorrow, but ask yourself whether you would still have taken this job if you'd already read this book and done the work I gave you to do.

Lastly, I'd like you to take stock of your mental and spiritual game. Are you taking the best care of your body and mind? Are you getting enough good sleep every night? (No, five hours isn't enough.) Are you really going offline while on vacation (assuming you're taking vacations) to recharge? Are you seeking mentors who can help you win the mental game? Are you doing something physical with your body at least five times a week? Do you have a spiritual practice?

At the end of the day, selling your way *in* to the life you really want won't be about the professional sales training your company sends you to, or the fact that you've mastered how to do the perfect software demo, or that you can handle objections with the best of them. It will be about how well you know yourself and how you invested in yourself. These are the difference makers-- the things that set the Top 10 Percenters apart from the rest.

26

The Work to Get to the Top Doesn't Happen at Work

f you could earn an additional $3M, $5M, or $10M in your lifetime, would you be willing to dedicate three to five hours a week to upping your game?

Of course you would. You just don't think it's possible.

If you think I'm kidding about those numbers, I'm not. If you're not reaching the Top 10 Percent of your profession, you are leaving a lot of money on the table.

"Income Math"

Let's start with the assumption that you dedicate thirty years of your life to selling.

Your **average** base salary over those thirty years is $60,000 = **$1,800,000**.

Your **average** commission percentage is 8 percent over those thirty years.

You sell $400,000 a year in your first ten years and $750,000 a year in your next twenty years (on **average**) so over thirty years, you sell $19,000,000 x 8 percent = **$1,520,000**

So as an **average** sales professional you'll make **$3,320,000** in those thirty years (for the purpose of this exercise we'll ignore inflation and pretend the government isn't taking a large percentage of your income for the purpose of this exercise).

- Average Base Salary: $1,800,000
- Average Commission/Bonus: $1,520,000
- Average Total: $3,320,000

Let's say that you dedicate thirty years of your life to sales *and* you spend fifteen of those years as a **Top 10 Percenter**. Now let's re-run the math:

Your **Top 10 Percenter** base salary over those thirty years is: $85,000 = **$2,550,000** (companies pay more for top talent).

Your **Top 10 Percenter** commission percentage is 10 percent over those thirty years (as a Top 10 Percenter, you'll reach the top of the commission scale and will get bonuses.)

You sell $500,000 a year in your first ten years and $1,000,000 a year in your next twenty years (on average) so over thirty years, you sell $25,000,000 x 11 percent = **$2,750,000**

- Top 10 Percenter Base salary = $2,550,000
- Top 10 Percenter Commission/Bonus = $2,750,000
- Top 10 Percenter Total = $5,300,000

Financial difference of being a Top 10 Percenter: ***$1,980,000***

How would an extra **$2 million dollars** change your life and that of your family?

The data don't lie (#Kristieism). Three to five hours a week really is all it takes. But here's the catch; those three to five hours don't happen "on the clock." I'm not talking about spending three to five hours doing more cold calling, prospecting, researching, or hobnobbing. I'm talking about spending three to five hours a week on your mental, physical, and spiritual game so you have the edge professionally when you're doing sales activities like cold calling, prospecting, researching, hobnobbing, and *selling*.

There are no lazy Rock Stars. In the book *Outliers* by Malcolm Gladwell, he writes that his research showed the very best in every field—from basketball stars like Lebron James to real Rock Stars like Mick Jagger—put in 10,000 hours of intense practice to reach mastery. As a competitive tennis player, I enjoy following a number of professional tennis players and understanding what makes them top competitors. One player in particular has had my attention for a few years: Novak Djokovic. I just watched Djokovic win the 2023 US Open Grand Slam at thirty-six years of age! He is now the oldest person to ever win a Grand Slam.

Djokovic first got my attention for his antics on the court—I appreciate a little bit of rebel in my idols—but what kept my attention was when I learned how much time and attention he spends on his mental, physical, and spiritual game to make his body perform like someone in their twenties.

I'm sure it won't come as a big surprise that Djokovic spends two to three hours a day practicing on the court, but here's how he ensures he is getting the most out of those practice sessions so, at thirty-six, he's ready to take on the likes of nineteen-year-old Ben Shelton and twenty-year-old Carlos Alcaraz.

Djokovic makes sure he gets eight to nine hours of sleep each night. He eats an almost exclusively plant-based diet. He starts each morning with a glass of warm water with lemon, to help his body detoxify. After that, he drinks celery juice followed by a green smoothie. He eats mostly fruits and veggies in the morning so his body doesn't have to expend any energy on digestion because he wants to make sure he has all the energy he needs for his practice sessions. His first meal of the day is a power bowl containing grains, fruit, nuts, almond milk, and honey (which has antibacterial properties.) His lunch is a complex-carb affair, usually including pasta and a salad. For dinner he will have another salad, pasta, and maybe a piece of salmon if he's got a match coming up the next day.

Djokovic isn't only committed to making his body a temple; he's committed to his physical, mental, and spiritual health as well. Here are a list of other tactics, strategies, and activities he's committed to, which he believes will get him to the top of the ATP tour and keep him there:

- Stretching: even before charity matches!
- Dynamic stretching to mimic his movements on the court.
- Foam-rolling: my least favorite post-match activity!
- Time in the Space Egg: this little-known machine is used by top athletes to increase oxygen absorption and aid in recovery.
- Training at high altitudes (he likes to hike in the mountains).
- Yoga: not only for flexibility, but he also practices the spiritual side of yoga, fifteen minutes of mindfulness practice each day.
- Breathwork
- Meditation
- Strength training

I know it's easy for a man whose total prize money is hovering around $175M to afford nutritionists, trainers, coaches, sports psychologists, physios, and a $100K Space Egg. But remember what I said about my choosing to have coaches, hypnotists, and therapists on my team? I don't do it because I can afford it, I can afford it because I made the investment *before* I could easily afford it. I know Djokovic didn't get to that $175M mark without investing both money and discipline. You can have all the resources in the world, but if you don't invest in your success and apply discipline, none of those resources and benefits will help you.

Would it really be that hard to listen to a sales podcast or business book on Audible instead of listening to music in the car? Could you go to bed at 10 p.m. instead of 11:30 p.m.? Could you start your day with a walk or meditation? Could you change one meal a day from processed foods to whole foods? Would you be willing to make some minor changes that could have a major impact on your income and your life, to the tune of $2,000,000?

I don't just want you to get to the top 10 percent, I want you to be able to enjoy it with those you love for years to come. Not to catastrophize, but are your eating, sleeping, and exercise habits (or lack thereof) not only keeping you from getting to the Top 10 Percent but also shortening your life and your total earning potential? Are you willing to trade $250,000 in earnings for a third glass of wine? Are you willing to give up $500,000 in income instead of walking three miles five times a week? For some of you, we're not talking about getting to the top 10 percent, we're talking about not seeing your kids graduate from college, not walking your daughter down the aisle, and not playing catch with your grandkids.

I mentioned earlier that Mick Jagger put in 10,000 hours of intense practice to reach mastery. Based on his 2013 biography titled, *Mick: The Wild Life and Mad Genius of Jagger*, you might be calling me out about the importance of the mental, physical, and spiritual game. True, the 60s Mick might not have been the poster child for health, but here's what he's been doing for years that has gotten him to eighty! Jagger's diet consists primarily of fresh fruit and veggies, whole grains, legumes, chicken, and fish. He also does regular interval training and is said to work out two to three hours a day! Many eighty-year-olds are sitting in front of the A/C, watching TV or playing cards in the game room of the nursing home. What Jaggar is doing daily requires discipline. I have a feeling he's intending to live a high-quality life for a long, long time.

Being a Rock Star sales rep is no different; if you want to earn at the top of the game you have to play at the top of the game. If you want to #ownyourownlife you have to live like a true Rock Star as well and that includes being disciplined.

If you've read this far you know there are a whole string of other #kristieisms that relate to doing the work outside of work.

- #ownyourownshit
- I can't motivate the unmotivated, but I can inspire the self-motivated.

- Help those who want to help themselves.
- Decisions are free, consequences are not.
- Do the right things, and the right things will happen.
- #SowtoGrow

Here's what all those #kristieisms add up to: if you want to be the person who makes it to the top, you don't stop doing the work just because the clock hits 5 p.m. or the calendar says it's a weekend.

You may remember that when I'm conducting interviews I always ask this question: "Name three things you do consistently, regardless of the job you have or the role you're in, that you think has led to your success."

I know I'm talking to a potential Top 10 Percenter when, without hesitation, they tell me about the things they're doing *outside* of work.

- I'm at the gym every morning by 6 a.m.
- I listen to sales podcasts weekly.
- I read a business or sales book each quarter.
- I have a spiritual practice.
- I put my phone down for two hours a day so I can be present for my family.
- I make sure I get eight hours of sleep each night.
- I write down my goals and have an accountability partner.
- I go to church each week.
- I have a group of friends, and we use each other as advisors or a personal board of directors.

Top 10 Percenters have not only mastered the sales skills needed to outperform and out-earn their co-workers and their competition; they also know there are other skills they must sharpen to stay at the top once they've arrived—skills that aren't even on the radar for the other 90 percent. And they're working on those skills on their own time.

The answers I shared here to that question, "Name three things you do consistently, regardless of the job you have or the role you're in, that you think has led to your success," are just some examples. Top performers build top performer habits (#Kristieism). So I know they will list at least one habit in each of these categories:

- Physical health: they have a schedule for how often they go to the gym, or take a walk, or work with a trainer, or do yoga ,and they're building habits that support their body such as sleep, relaxation, and nutrition.
- Relationships: they regularly spend quality time with people they love, they have professional groups and networks, they have social habits that keep them connected with a wider community.
- Learning: they have habits that build their personal development as well as their professional knowledge, and they're investing in having an active brain and staying in learning mode.
- Mental/Spiritual: they're consistent in their "inner work" through meditation, prayer, journaling, church, or other spiritual groups.

Top 10 Percenters know they won't perform at their best if they're only getting five hours of sleep a night, eating poorly, and can't climb a flight of stairs without stopping at the top to catch their breath. They need their body, mind, and spirit to be just as sharp as their professional sales skills. And they know the most important work they do to get to the top isn't happening "on the clock."

27

My Job Is Done. Now Yours Begins

You remember early in the book I shared this #kristieism: "There are jobs where you have a set income and jobs where you set your own income."

Also, if you remember, I ended it with "It's your choice."

I'm going to end our time together here the same way I usually end trainings and keynote speeches. It goes something like this:

*So what do Top 10 Percenters know that others haven't figured out yet? That the work to get to the top doesn't take place **at** work. It takes place **after** work. It takes place on their drive home from the office; it takes place after the kids go to bed; it takes place while they're working on their short game, and it takes place when they spend time with others like them because Top 10 Percenters know, that their circle matters.*

Now it's time to get real. Here's the question you should be asking yourself. "Am I willing to do the work outside of work that others are not willing to do so I can join the very exclusive Top 10 Percenter's Club?"

And that's really the only question you need to be asking yourself. Are you willing, will you *choose*, to put everything I've shared here to work for you? Will you choose to do the work to know yourself, to master the sales knowledge framework, and to build the habits and invest the discipline and resources to take your place at the top?

If you're already screaming, "YES!" and are truly committed, then let me tell you what I think will happen next. You'll grab the notes you've taken and the workbook you've filled out as you've read or listened to this book and you're going to go back to the beginning and hone the plan you've begun crafting.

You're going to gather your inner circle, or start building your inner circle, and you're going to share your goals and intentions and ask them to be your cheerleaders and accountability partners.

You're going to make mental, spiritual, and physical changes in your life that will ensure you can not only get to the top but that you'll stay there.

You're going to develop the discipline it takes to put your personal plan in motion, be held accountable to that plan, and make the necessary changes to your spiritual, mental, and physical game so you're always able to hit your PR (personal record).

And here's one more thing I know. You can do it. You're going to reach the Top 10 Percent in your industry, company, or among your peer group.

You *can* sell your way into the life you really want to live and deserve to have.

Acknowledgments

I often tell people that I live a blessed life, and I believe that. I also believe there have been so many people along my journey who put me on the path I'm on today and not having encountered even one of those people might have altered my trajectory.

I never wanted to write a book. What I wanted was to have more opportunities to speak and share my sales wisdom with more sales professionals and touch more lives. In 2019, while walking to lunch with Barbara Weaver Smith, at my first Women Sales Pros Shebang conference, she told me if I wanted to speak, then I'd have to write a book. I remember my immediate reaction.

"That ticks me off," I told her. "I've got important sh*t to say, and I shouldn't have to write a book to share it with people."

She looked at me straight in the eye and said, "Well that's the way it works." So you wouldn't have read or listened to *Selling Your Way IN* if it hadn't been for Barbara telling me like it is and me trusting that she knew a few things about writing books—she is the best-selling author of *Whale Hunting: How to Land Big Sales and Transform Your Company*—and that I should listen to her. Thank you, Barbara, for being honest and direct that day and then spending the next year mentoring me through the pandemic.

The journey to writing this book really started in 2000 when I made the decision to leave my job with a Fortune 500 company and join a company with fewer than fifteen employees to work for a man I barely knew in an industry I absolutely didn't know anything about (B2B subscription model? What's that?). That one decision to go to work for Dean Pichee at Business Training Library (BTL then and now Bizlibrary) changed my life. At the time, I thought I was the one taking a huge risk. Now I know it was the other way around. Over those ten years, Dean taught me about people, process, product, profits, and what good wine tasted like. Together we worked hard, played hard, and grew his $1M company into something we were both proud of and that afforded us both a much better life than we'd had in 2000. Dean, thank you for taking a chance on me, for believing that I had something to offer you and your company, and for your friendship over the years. I grew more in those ten years than in any other period of my life. Grateful is an understatement.

All roads lead back to Dean and that's how I met David Friedman. David, thank you for being my business sugar daddy! You gave me more than just financial support. You gave me the confidence that I really could start my own business. You were so excited that you started working on a name and logo for my business before I'd even wrapped my head around the concept. Every time I see the "Jonesing for Sales" brand and logo at the top of my monthly newsletter, I think of you. Thank you for your belief in me, your encouragement, and friendship going back twenty-plus years.

Thank you to John True for introducing me to client #1, Observable Networks! That introduction and meeting was the spark that set off a wildfire that is now my life. Nine years later you still provide introductions to companies you think could benefit from my help, and I continue to be appreciative. More than that, I am thankful for the friendship that developed.

To Mike Weinberg, whom I met not by chance but by Universal conspiracy. Your giving and kindness know no boundaries. Not only did you help me secure client #3, but you graciously agreed to mentor me throughout my first year in business as you were simultaneously watching your own business take off like a rocket ship. You shared your contract with me, you took my calls while you were on the road, and you didn't rub it in when my Jayhawks lost in the Sweet 16 more years than I care to remember. I was beyond humbled when you agreed to write the foreword for this book and was filled with pride and joy after I read it. Thank you for all your support over the years. It's meant the world to me.

If it was Barbara Weaver Smith who provided the tough love to start me down the path to writing this book, it was Dixie Gillaspie who picked up the ball from her and helped make sure I made it to the finish line. Dixie's expertise, advice, compassion, encouragement, support, and, God knows, barrels full of patience made this experience enjoyable and rewarding. The book *we've* created is one I'm so proud of, and I could not have done it without you. Thank you for the hours and hours you poured into me and this book, for the friendship that we've grown, and for always knowing what to say in the moments I felt lost. You knew what I didn't, that not only could I write a book but that I could write from my heart and in doing so impact the lives of sales professionals looking to have a more fulfilling career and life.

There are so many others who have provided support, encouragement, and have been on this journey with me.

Thank you to the best tennis fivesome any girl could ask for (Susan, Renee, Chris, Sunita, and Linda). You all have been there in the best of times and the worst of times, and I love you!

Thank you to Logan for providing content for the book (naturally curious) and for letting me know, on occasion, that something I've done is "Fire!" You're my world. I love you and cherish you.

Lastly, I want to thank all the sales professionals I've had the pleasure to work with over the years. Not only did you inspire this book, but you also taught me so much along the way. Those early years were rough as I tried to figure out so many things about B2B sales, prospecting, objection handling, and closing deals. Your need for coaching, mentoring, and training made me a better sales leader, coach, and consultant. Kristieisms wouldn't exist if it weren't for you!

ABOUT THE AUTHOR

Kristie K. Jones brings over twenty years of experience as a sales leader, during which she has hired, coached, and trained nearly 650 sales representatives. Her experience spans a range of sales leadership positions, from retail to software sales. Since founding Sales Acceleration Group in 2016, she has served as a sales process strategist, sales coach, hiring consultant, speaker, and executive coach, assisting founders, CEOs, owners, sales leaders, and sales professionals in enhancing their sales processes, strategies, skills, and team to boost revenues.

Kristie's "take no prisoners" approach has made her indispensable for companies aiming to instill discipline and foster a culture of accountability. Her direct communication style, combined with years of driving impressive sales results, led to Udemy tapping her to create their first elearning course on sales prospecting for their Udemy for Business division. Additionally, she was invited to join the Sales Experts Channel as an instructor and regularly contributes to the UK's *Top Sales Magazine*.

Audiences find Kristie's presentations engaging and packed with passion, energy, and valuable insights, causing them to nod enthusiastically and take notes furiously. She has been featured in various publications and podcasts and has had her own billboard on the NASDAQ building in Times Square. With a deep passion for helping sales professionals, Kristie's guiding philosophies of #ownyourownshit and #ownyourownincome inspire a culture of accountability and respect in every client she serves. Kristie currently resides in St. Louis, Missouri.

Let's Stay Connected

Thank you for reading *Selling Your Way IN*. I'm honored that you trusted me to help you get to the Top 10 Percent, so that you can own your income and own your life.

Selling your way in and owning your income will be a journey, not an event. As such, I want to continue to provide you support throughout your journey.

Ways to stay connected:

Sign up for my e-newsletter at: kristiekjones.com/join

Visit my blog: kristiekjones.com/blog

Connect with me on LinkedIn: linkedin.com/in/kristiekjones

Follow me on Instagram: instagram.com/kristiejones.sales

Subscribe to my YouTube Channel: youtube.com/@kristiekjones

Leaving a review

If you found the book valuable, please leave a review on the online retailer's website where you purchased the book. Reviews not only support the book, but they are helpful for those who are in search of help taking their career to the next level.

Thank you,
Kristie

A free ebook edition
is available with the
purchase of this book.

To claim your free ebook edition:

1. Visit MorganJamesBOGO.com
2. Sign your name CLEARLY in the space
3. Complete the form and submit a photo of
   the entire copyright page
4. You or your friend can download the ebook
   to your preferred device

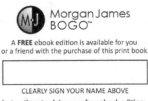

Morgan James
BOGO™

A **FREE** ebook edition is available for you
or a friend with the purchase of this print book.

CLEARLY SIGN YOUR NAME ABOVE

Instructions to claim your free ebook edition:
1. Visit MorganJamesBOGO.com
2. Sign your name CLEARLY in the space above
3. Complete the form and submit a photo
   of this entire page
4. You or your friend can download the ebook
   to your preferred device

Print & Digital Together Forever.

Snap a photo

Free ebook

Read anywhere